# First Draft
## in 30 Days

a novel writer's system for building
a complete and cohesive manuscript

# First Draft in 30 Days

## a novel writer's system for building a complete and cohesive manuscript

**WRITER'S DIGEST BOOKS**
Cincinnati, Ohio
www.writersdigest.com

## Karen S. Wiesner

Visit our Web site at www.writersdigest.com for information on more resources for writers.

To receive a free weekly e-mail newsletter delivering tips and updates about writing and about Writer's Digest products, register directly at our Web site at http://newsletters.fwpublications.com.

10   09   08   07   06      7   6   5   4   3

**Library of Congress Cataloging-in-Publication Data**

Wiesner, Karen
   First draft in 30 days : a novel writer's system for building a complete and cohesive manuscript / Karen Wiesner—1st ed.
     p.   cm.
   Includes index.
   ISBN-13: 978-1-58297-296-1 (alk. paper)
   ISBN-10: 1-58297-296-6 (alk. paper)
    1. Fiction—Authorship. 2. Manuuscript preparation (Authorship). I. Title: First draft in thirty days. II. Title.

PN3365.W56   2005
808.3—dc22                                                                                    2004062032
                                           CIP

Edited by Kelly Nickell
Designed by Terri Eubanks
Cover designed by Claudean Wheeler
Production coordinated by Robin Richie

## My Thanks

While I'd love to claim this book was borne entirely out of my own wisdom, alas, I'll concede to having quite a few generous hands that helped sand off all the rough edges:

Kelly Nickell, my fantastic editor at Writer's Digest Book, who helped me develop this method in a way that makes sense to more than just myself!

Marshall Cook, writers' reference author extraordinaire, as well as my mentor on one of the earliest forms of this project. Thanks for helping me put together the proposal the first time around, then agreeing to critique, review it, and review it again.

Christine DeSmet, a fellow writer and friend who graciously agreed to give the book an advance review. I can't thank you enough for all your invaluable suggestions, Chris.

Christine Spindler, who believed in this book from the very first time I ever mentioned it online (back in the days when it was simply an ambitious idea so many others shot down as too lofty). May our writing partnership flourish for many long years.

The WisRWA authors who allowed me to give a "mini workshop" of this method at their retreat before I'd ever written the book.

And, finally, to my sister, Linda Derkez, with whom my desire to be a writer grew to the point that nothing else would ever do.

## About the Author

Karen Wiesner is the award-winning author of more than twenty books, including *Sweet Dreams*, *Waiting for an Eclipse* (Book II of the Wounded Warrior Series), and *Mirror, Mirror* (Book III of the Wounded Warrior Series). Her novels cover such diverse genres as romance, mystery/police procedural, suspense, thriller, paranormal, and action/adventure titles. She also writes children's books and poetry. Her previous writing reference titles focused on nonsubsidy, royalty-paying electronic publishing, and author promotion. Karen is a member of Jewels of the Quill, RWA, EPIC, Sisters in Crime, and BooksWeLove.net. She lives in Wisconsin with her long-suffering husband and son.

For more information about Karen and her work, visit her Web sites at www.karenwiesner.com and www.falconsbend.com.

# First Draft **in 30 Days**

## TABLE OF CONTENTS

# Making the 30-Day Method Work for You

*Credit belongs to . . . the man who actually strives to do the deeds, who knows the great enthusiasm and knows the great devotion, who spends himself on a worthy cause, who, at best, knows in the end the triumph of great achievement. And who, at worst, if he fails, at least fails while daring greatly . . .*

*—Teddy Roosevelt*

Imagine you could write the first draft of a novel in only thirty days. Imagine you could figure out how long it would take to complete each step *down to the day*—that you could set accurate goals that would allow you to maintain a constant momentum in your writing career. Imagine writing quality novels—*each and every time*—that no editor in his right mind could turn down. Everything you need is within your grasp. As you complete the 30-day method explained in this book, you're going to discover much about yourself and your abilities.

My 30-day method for outlining a novel eliminates many of the problems that plague fiction writers. Why dig for plots blindly when, with a little preparation, you can craft something worthwhile from start to finish? Why go through countless, lengthy drafts of a novel when you can create an outline so complete that it actually qualifies as the first draft? Why revise hundreds of pages of a complicated manuscript when you can revise a snapshot of your novel that's a quarter of the novel's length? Using an outline can *significantly* reduce the time it takes you to complete a project from start to finish—sometimes by more than half.

The method contained in *First Draft in 30 Days* will work for any genre of fiction. The method is good for any type of writer, whether you've just started writing or you've been at it for twenty-five years. It will work for you if you want clear direction from start to finish, and it will work for you if you simply want to use parts of the system to enhance your own way of writing. It will work for you if you are already productive and successful but yearn to take the world by storm.

You may be under the mistaken impression that using an outline stifles creativity, that you can't be productive in every aspect of your writing life. If you've never worked with an outline before or prefer a more leisurely method of working as you embark on what you see as a spiritual journey, adhering to this structured process may sound downright impossible—and in some cases, even horrifying. As you'll see, there's no *wrong* way to write a book—but there are *ineffective* ways of writing. Only you can decide if this method is for you. If you're not sure, try this method once (though it's best to try it at least two or three times) and see if it makes a big difference in what you're able to accomplish.

## THE GOAL OF THE 30-DAY METHOD

The outline you'll complete using the 30-day method will become a snapshot of your novel. After finishing a full outline, you should feel two things: (1) that you've got the makings of an entire book (your story should feel complete, solid, exciting, and wholly satisfying) and (2) that you still desperately want to write the book you've outlined.

A first draft *outline* completed using the 30-day method is equivalent to the first draft of a *manuscript*. Because you've revised it so thoroughly, it reads with all the completeness and excitement of a finished novel. Using your outline as you write the first draft of your book (which, in almost all cases, will be the *final* draft, needing only minor editing and polishing) should be so easy, you might even feel a little guilty about it. You will have done all the hard work creating the outline.

Throughout this book, we'll work on the assumption that the first draft of your book isn't a fully completed draft in the traditional sense, but instead a comprehensive outline—your first, whole glimpse of the book and a snapshot of what it will be once finished. The outline you create over the next thirty days will become the foundation upon which your entire novel will come to rest. This method is a way to lay out the full course of the story as it flows from beginning to end. Your first draft is in *outline* form, not yet a fully realized manuscript. The first time you sit down to begin the actual writing process, you'll create your second—and in some cases, *final*—draft. (I also call this your first *full* draft.)

## YOUR COMMITMENT TO THE 30-DAY METHOD

Despite its flexibility, the 30-day method requires a great deal of commitment from you as a writer. The first thing you need in order to become a productive writer is self-discipline. This method will give that to you in spades—if you're willing to dedicate yourself to doing your part. I won't pull any punches with you: Not everyone will be able to complete a first draft outline in exactly thirty days on the first try. Does that mean you'll never be able to do it? No, it doesn't mean that at all. This method, like all methods, requires a sufficient amount of practice. The *longer* you use it, the *more* you use it, the more time and effort you'll eventually shave off your outlining schedule. In the future, you may even notice it takes you considerably less time to write the first full draft of your book.

Does it mean you've failed if it takes you ninety days instead of thirty? Of course not. If you need more (or less) time to perform certain steps in the process, you can adjust your schedule easily. But this method will probably make you work harder than you've ever worked before. Some will enjoy the challenge. Others will use the method while setting their own deadlines for each step. And still others won't be willing to allow their muse to be harnessed in this way. Find what works for you over the long haul, not simply for the moment. Even if you find the next thirty days difficult, I encourage you to continue using this method for all of your projects. I promise you it will get easier with experience.

## HOW TO USE THIS BOOK

*First Draft in 30 Days* is broken down into ten chapters followed by four appendices. In chapter one we'll discuss the various schedules that make up the 30-day method and its six crucial stages. We'll also explore some brainstorming techniques because brainstorming is an essential part of this entire process.

Chapters two through seven will take you step by step through the six principle stages of the 30-day method. Each stage is broken down into a certain number of days during which different segments of your outline will be developed, combined, and revised. Each chapter starts with a review of the schedule and prepares you for the work ahead.

If you already have a completed manuscript, you may want to read chapter eight before reading chapters two through seven. This chapter will show you how to use the 30-day method to outline an already completed manuscript. By going back and outlining your completed manuscript, you can build on its strengths and eliminate its weaknesses, since the process of outlining will show you exactly where the story needs work.

Chapter nine will take you through the process of using your completed outline to write your manuscript. It will also discuss how to use writing and revision schedule sheets to keep yourself on track.

Chapter ten will show you how the structuring concepts of the 30-day method can also be used to shape your career. In addition, you'll learn how to use goal sheets to stay focused on each of your projects.

The four appendices contain all the supplemental materials you'll need to work your way through the 30-day method:

*Appendix A* contains a glossary that includes key outlining terms discussed within this book. If you ever get confused about what a term means, just consult the glossary.

*Appendix B* contains all the schedules necessary to complete the 30-day method for a new book idea or for one already in some form of development. Overview and step-by-step schedules are included as well. The schedules contain columns where you can include specific dates and notes for yourself as you work.

*Appendix C* contains the worksheets referenced in chapters two through nine. (In those chapters you'll see completed worksheet samples based on what some of today's bestsellers may have looked like in outline form.)

*Appendix D* includes the career goal sheets discussed in chapter ten.

## UNDERSTANDING THE 30-DAY METHOD SCHEDULE

We'll discuss the 30-day method schedules again and again throughout this book. Understanding what's happening on each day of the process will help you to stay focused and on track over the next thirty days. Keep in mind that as you become more experienced with outlining, you'll be able to make adjustments to the method and individualize it to best suit your needs.

Let's take a look at the overall schedule behind the 30-day method.

| Schedule | Stages To Complete | Days Required |
|---|---|---|
| **Days 1–6** | **Stage 1:** Preliminary Outline | 6 |
| **Days 7–13** | **Stage 2:** Research | 7 |
| **Days 14–15** | **Stage 3:** Story Evolution | 2 |
| **Days 16–24** | **Stage 4:** Formatted Outline | 9 |
| **Days 25–28** | **Stage 5:** Outline Evaluation | 4 |
| **Days 29–30** | **Stage 6:** Revise the Outline | 2 |

This is simply an overview of each stage. Keep in mind that each of the six stages identified above has its own day-to-day schedule. These individual schedules are discussed at length at the start of each corresponding chapter.

The first couple of times you use this method, you may find yourself struggling to stay on schedule. Don't worry if you need to allow yourself an extra day or two for some tasks. As you become more familiar with the method, you'll find it easier to stay on schedule.

While this method is specifically designed with the promise of completing a full outline before you begin writing the book, we'll talk about outlining and writing in tandem in chapter five, in case you find that you work better that way.

Please remember that the first steps in creating a comprehensive outline are very rough—each step will build on the previous one. The preliminary outline you create in Stage 1 won't contain everything. You'll just be getting your basics down at this point. With each step, you'll be developing more details about every aspect of the book, and your outline will grow to reflect that.

As you're writing the first full draft of your book, you'll also be re-evaluating your outline periodically as your story takes on a life of its own and moves in directions you might not have planned. You won't stop evaluating the strength of your outline until the book is complete.

## WHAT YOU'LL NEED

In order to use this book, you'll need to have access to the basics: pens, paper, paperclips, a stapler, and even scissors. You also may find it helpful to have expanding and two-pocket folders on hand to help you keep everything organized.

The 30-day method can be completed using pens and paper or on a computer. If you use a computer, it's easiest to start a new document for most of the stages in the preliminary outline phase and to save each document to the same project folder. Also, always remember to print a clean copy of your document at the end of the day. Doing so will keep you better organized and may just inspire a little brainstorming.

## CREATIVITY AND OUTLINES

Before I tried writing an outline, I believed I simply couldn't learn to use one. Then I forced myself to try using an outline—my own version of an outline—for a novel I'd already written numerous drafts of. First I sketched out a couple of chapters, and then I started writing the book once more. I completed the outline about midway through writing the first draft of the book. Not long after that, when I first used an outline for a brand new project, I found myself brainstorming constantly and productively. I was able to outline six to eight scenes of the book without writing a word of the actual novel.

Since this meant that the outline was completed well ahead of the novel, I was able to revise the *outline* instead of the *novel*. A wondrous thing happened in this process: I saw the entire novel from start to finish condensed in one place—including all the unworkable parts. All I had to do to strengthen the entire *book* was fix the unworkable elements in the *outline*.

Now when I write a novel, I always start with a complete outline that I can revise as many times as I need to. Writing a book has almost become a simple process. After outlining, most projects require only one full draft and a final edit and polish. I save time, effort, and many, many intense rewrites. I can also write more "final draft" novels a year, which means I have more to show for myself at the end of the year than a half dozen book drafts that need yet another overhaul.

I'll be the first to state emphatically that there is no wrong way to write a book. I've talked to hundreds of authors, published and unpublished, and all of them have their own unique ways of working. There's no *wrong* way, but some are less effective than others.

Sadly, too many authors believe outlines are a last resort. They see writing as a magical series of epiphanies that somehow takes them from the first page of a novel to the last with little or no premeditation. I don't discount the magical element—because it *is* there in some degree—but I simply can't buy into the spiritual intuition way of writing. For one thing, not every brand-new, never-written-much-or-anything-before writer can be expected to have this kind of intuition. Any writer—experienced or not—who finds it difficult to develop plot and character as she writes can benefit from a structured outlining process.

Author John Berendt says, "Don't make an outline; make a laundry list. The very idea of an outline suggests rigidity; items on a laundry list can be shifted around. Don't lock the structure in too early. A piece of writing should evolve as it's being written." I hear the same thing from almost every writer I talk to, whether or not he's published: Writers like outlines about as much as a homeowner likes termites. The word can actually make some writers cringe and do a full-body shudder. An outline sounds like too much work; it's uninspiring, too confining, absolutely unappealing, necessitates the ability to see far ahead in a novel, *I can't possibly work that way*!

Writers who haven't tried an outlining system have many questions about the process: Is it possible for an outline to be flexible? To take into account my individuality as a writer? Can I continue to be creative using an outline? Can I use an outline for writing in any fiction genre? Can using an outline reduce the number of rewrites I have to do? Can it really take me *less* time to complete a project from start to finish using an outline? Won't setting goals clip my wings rather than allow me to stretch them?

Despite their abhorrence of the word *outline*, many authors are seeking a method to give them direction, a method that embraces an individual's way of working, a method that takes away none of the joy of creating. They want something that will streamline the process and make them more productive, so they're not surrounding themselves with half-finished projects and manuscripts in need of major revisions.

If you are one of these authors, let me assure you: An outline *can* be flexible, *can* be so complete it actually qualifies as the first draft of the novel. An outline can make it possible for writers like you to achieve more with less work, not only reducing the number of drafts required for each project, but perhaps even reducing the number to a single draft. This means producing more books and quite likely making more sales to publishers.

Instead of viewing an outline as an inflexible, unchangeable hindrance, imagine it as a snapshot of a novel. A snapshot that captures everything the novel will contain, but on a much smaller scale. Just as a photograph can be touched up, this snapshot of a novel can be adjusted and rearranged until it's smooth, strong, and breathtakingly exciting. Revising a comprehensive outline of your novel means revising fifty to a hundred pages instead of four times that. You must admit, my fellow writer, that an outline offers many benefits.

Without robbing you of the joy of your craft, *First Draft in 30 Days* teaches you how to become a systematic, self-disciplined, productive author—no matter your genre or level of experience. While the technique behind the 30-day method takes into account that you're an individual and may have your own methods of getting from Point A to Point B, it nonetheless helps clarify your vision of your story before you begin writing your first (and possibly final) full draft. No more wasted time or endless overhauls and revisions. The clearer your vision of the story before you start the actual writing, the more fleshed out the story will be once it makes it to paper.

## IMPROVING YOUR PRODUCTIVITY

The method contained in this book, combined with the goal-setting suggestions in chapter ten, should cut in half the time it usually takes you to complete a project from outline to final draft. Of course, each writer is different and works at different speeds. A longer book will certainly take longer to write. However, a more complex story won't increase your writing time because you will work out the kinks of the story while outlining.

Before I started using the 30-day method, I could write a full draft of a novel in about two months—not counting all the time that I lost when my inspiration failed and I set the book aside and started a new one before eventually returning to the first one. It's also important to note that early in my writing career, I required *twelve drafts* per book to get something halfway decent. Later, by using my earlier drafts but not yet using an outline, I got that number down to four drafts per book. Do the math yourself: When I needed twelve drafts per book, it took me two years or more to complete one novel. When I needed four drafts per book, it took eight months to complete a novel.

Since I've been using the full outline process, the most time it takes to complete an outline of a book—regardless of length—is two to three weeks. And it only takes me one to two months to complete a first and final manuscript draft.

With each book you complete, your skills as a writer are likely to improve. You'll also increase your chances of making a sale if you have more than one book to shop around to publishers and agents.

## SEE THE 30-DAY METHOD IN ACTION

In this book, I use a wide variety of examples to demonstrate each step of the 30-day method. Inspired by best-selling novels, these examples come from a variety of genres. They will show you just how versatile the *First Draft in 30 Days* method is. You can use it for every single genre of fiction, no matter how short or long your work is.

However, it's equally important that you see the method used on a single book, the way you'll start out using it yourself. To this end, I want to encourage you to visit my Web site, where you'll find examples of each step in the process taken from a single book. Included are all the worksheets in Appendix C as I completed them for my novel *Sweet Dreams*. You'll also find the full outline of the book, including an excerpt to show you how the bones took on flesh. Seeing a cohesive picture of how the method works through every stage of my novel will help you visualize how it works as you use it for your novel. Just click on "First Draft" at www.karenwiesner.com.

## GETTING STARTED

The 30-day outlining process described in this book can allow you to harness your muse and put her to work so that you can become a more productive writer. You may feel that by harnessing your muse, you risk restricting your source of inspiration and creativity. Fear not. The 30-day method merely directs your creativity so you can complete your writing projects quickly and easily.

If you're willing to take a leap of faith and commit yourself for the long haul, turn the page and let's get started!

# CHAPTER 1

# Brainstorming Before You Outline

There are so many skills crucial to a writer's success that it's often easy to overlook one of the most basic and necessary skills of all: brainstorming. Brainstorming, an exercise that's especially important when starting a new project, is invaluable when it comes to maintaining the ambition and focus necessary to complete a project. As you outline using the 30-day method, you'll focus your brainstorming so the process will be even more inspiring and productive.

## THE CREATIVE COFFEEPOT

I truly believe I've been a writer all my life, even before I put my first words on a page. I'm sure a lot of other authors feel this way, too. We writers spin fantasies in our heads, and this is where the majority of our work is done. Most of us have one thing in common: We come up with ideas in a chaotic, nonlinear way. We do it naturally and instinctively. I can't remember a day I wasn't daydreaming as a kid. My teachers throughout high school reported that I constantly had my head in the clouds.

Actually, I had my head in a *coffeepot*. You see, I've always likened the process of writing to brewing coffee in a percolator. The stories inside my head are in a creative coffeepot, brewing away. In the percolation stage of the writing process, stories come to life in large or small spurts: a sketch of a character or two, setting descriptions, some vague or definite plotline or action scene, glimmers of specific relationships, maybe even a few conversations. Most of it wouldn't make sense to anyone except me. When a story idea is constantly boiling up, it's time to put it into outline form and puzzle it out.

*Constant brainstorming, or brewing, is the most important part of writing an outline or a book.* No writing system, technique, or tool will work for you—not even the 30-day method—if you're not brainstorming constantly during a project. I can't emphasize that enough. You must brainstorm from the beginning of a project—before you even write a word of it—through the outlining, the writing, and the final edit and polish. You're in the car, running some errands—brainstorm. You're peeling potatoes for dinner—brainstorm. You're doing a mindless activity at work—brainstorm. My favorite place to brainstorm is in the car on a long drive, alone. I bring along a recording of music I've put together as a soundtrack for the book I'm brainstorming and let it transport me into the world I want to create. Do whatever you have to do to keep your story brewing furiously inside your creative coffeepot.

I recommend that you start brainstorming days, weeks, months, or even *years* before you begin work on a story. The best possible scenario, of course, is brainstorming years before you begin, jotting down notes as they come to you and putting them into their own folders.

I'm sure I'm not the only author who has at least fifty different stories percolating at any given time. Keeping them all straight becomes harder the older I get, and that's why it's so important to have some method for organizing it all.

Now is the time to create project folders for all of your strongest story ideas, even those you may not write for years. Write the title of each book on the front of its own two-pocket folder, then transfer all your notes (including any outlining and writing you've done on a story—anything that you might need or use) into the folders. If you've never formally written anything about this particular idea, having a folder for it will encourage you to brainstorm on the story. Keep all the project folders together in an accessible area of your office. In the future, put all your brainstorming notes directly into the appropriate folder. I keep all of my folders in one cabinet, which I call my story cupboard.

## Brewing (and Performing an Exorcism)

I read a long time ago about a best-selling author who always has more than one manuscript going at once. When he temporarily loses inspiration for one, he moves to another work in progress (hereafter referred to as WIP).

Jumping from project to project may be an effective way to work for some writers, but it can prevent you from making significant progress with any one project. At one point in my career I was juggling several ideas at a time, writing notes, starting stories—and not getting more than a few chapters written of each.

Most writers can't concentrate on more than one story at a time if they want to move forward steadily. New story ideas won't distract you if they're percolating gently on a back burner, but eventually, each of those ideas will brew to the point they're ready to be poured out on paper. This is natural—you want this to happen. But if you're trying to make headway with one project when another suddenly commands your attention, you need to find a way to set the new idea aside and refocus your concentration on your current project. You can do this by writing out notes on the new idea by hand (I'll explain why I recommend writing longhand in chapter eight) and relegating the idea to its own project folder, which you can pick up and review at a more convenient time. By purging the idea to paper, you effectively exorcise it so you can concentrate fully on your current WIP. (Even though I think of brainstorming as a brewing process, I consider purging an idea to paper as an exorcism—the metaphors the brain constructs for its own use aren't as tidy as the ones we construct for our readers.)

I have a separate folder for each of my story ideas, and I keep them all together in my story cupboard. If I need to purge an idea, I can simply pull out the folder for that story. Purging the idea is a quick process because my notes are usually only enough to fill a sticky note or a single sheet of paper. Occasionally, I do have to take a little more time to purge (a day or two) because the story has progressed fully to the pouring and puzzling out stage. The outline is forming rapidly in my head, and I have everything I need to put it together. Sometimes the only way to exorcise a particular story is to write down all the notes that come to me until I'm stalled or temporarily free of it. These go into the appropriate project folder. The story is then returned to the percolator, and I get back to my WIP.

Exorcise new story ideas whenever necessary so you can stay focused on your current WIP.

## BRAINSTORMING PRODUCTIVELY

I firmly believe that creative writing is 75 percent brewing, 25 percent actual writing. Some writers are so mentally involved with their stories that brainstorming takes the form of "mini-movies" reeling through their heads. These can be called up at will or with a little prompting, fast-forwarded, rewound, edited, then replayed. Turning the movies off can sometimes be impossible. Your brainstorming techniques may not include mini-movies, but the lesson is the same. Regardless of your brainstorming style, the process should be so inspirational and second-nature that you have difficulty shutting it down. While this can be darned inconvenient at times, it's absolutely necessary for every writer during both the outlining and writing stages.

Don't try to rein in or discipline your brainstorming—no matter how inconvenient it is. Brainstorming is what turns an average story into an extraordinary one. It's the magical element every author marvels about in the process of completing a book. Brainstorm day and night, whatever you do, wherever you are, whenever you possibly can.

Keeping the outline, the story in general, or specific scenes in your mind throughout the day untangles basic groundwork issues like timelines, certain events, character relationships, and all of the threads of a story (more about these later). At times, you may even work out whole conversations in your head. When it comes time to outline and write, fleshing out these scenes will be very simple.

Every author covets the ability to sit down to a blank screen or paper and begin to work immediately. The secret is brainstorming! When you brainstorm constantly and productively during both the outlining and writing processes, you will always be fully prepared to begin writing—without agonizing over the starting sentence or paragraph.

Notice I specified that you must brainstorm *productively* if you want the writing process to go smoothly and quickly. That's where your outline comes in. The brainstorming process will have allowed you to do all the hard work of plotting, characterization, etc., while creating your outline. Once you have an outline, you will know every single day what you'll be writing about in your book. You won't have to decide where the story is going as you write, because you'll have done all that in the outlining stage. The day or week *before* you begin actually writing a certain scene, start brainstorming selectively on that scene. This makes it that much easier to sit down and begin work immediately when the time comes. If you haven't spent enough time brainstorming on the coming scene, you'll have a difficult time when you sit down to write for the day.

There will be times when you find yourself mentally blocked, unable to puzzle out a certain idea. If you need help lighting the fire under your creative coffeepot, try some of the suggestions listed below:

1. Read a book or watch a movie in the same genre as your current project to create a springboard for your own brainstorming about adventurers, new worlds, quests, revolutions, romances, and battles.

2. Make a soundtrack for your current project. Choose songs that fit specific parts of your book or the theme of the whole book. Each time you hear a song from your soundtrack, it will inspire you to brainstorm on that project.

3. Take a long, slow, scenic drive alone. Bring along the soundtrack for your current project. If you think you'll have trouble remembering your thoughts when you get back home, take along a personal recorder. (Since you'll be brainstorming and possibly recording notes on your drive, make sure you drive slowly on a quiet, familiar road.)

4. Go on a long, slow walk alone. Enjoy nature and the particular season. Listen to your project soundtrack through headphones.

5. Soak in a hot bubble bath with your soundtrack and a glass of wine.

6. Go shopping. Buy yourself something your main character would like. If you've given your main character some kind of special possession or memento, buy something similar.

7. Get out of the house—go anywhere—and people-watch. Surreptitiously observe those around you to get ideas from gestures, movements, hints of an overheard conversation, or even just the way people look.

8. Work in the garden. Plant flowers or a tree. Physically planting and working the soil can help you mentally sow and nurture the seeds of creativity.

9. Ask yourself "what if?" questions about your plot and characters.

10. Try throwing unique ideas into your plot to see where they might lead in the outline.

11. Take a nap. You can be at your most creative while in the twilight state between awake and asleep.

12. Talk to anyone who'll listen to you about your story. This will not only help you form the story more clearly in your mind, but show you weak or interesting angles of your plot you hadn't considered before. (See the further discussion of verbal brainstorming below.)

13. Collect magazines, then cut out pictures of people and settings that resemble those in your story. (These will come in handy when you create character and setting sketches in the next chapter.) Clip articles about murders or strange and interesting events from newspapers or tabloids and save them for use when you need idea boosts.

14. Write with a partner on separate projects, in the same room. Then read what you've written to each other, not necessarily to critique so much as to uplift and energize your muse.

15. Write a letter to one of your characters (either from you or from another character in your story) just to see where it'll take you, or interview one or more of your characters.

16. Spend a weekend at a nice hotel or resort alone and write. Without the distractions of daily life at home, you may be able to write and brainstorm faster and more clearly.

17. Make yourself a cup of coffee or hot chocolate. The smell of coffee brewing always revs up my mind for writing.

18. If you write on a computer, try writing with pen and paper instead, or vice versa. Try putting each scene in your outline on an index card and playing with the chronological order.

19. List your main character's areas of interest (work and hobbies) and do something creative in one of these areas, like woodworking or flower arranging.

20. Interview someone in a career shared by one of your main characters.

21. Exercise while listening to your project's soundtrack.

22. If your book is set in a place other than where you live (and you can afford it), visit this setting. Seeing it in person may well inspire new directions for your story.

23. Establish a special room or area where you can write without interruptions or distractions. Or, in nice weather, make yourself a mobile office in the backyard or a local park.

24. Research a subject for the book, either via the Internet or a library. What you discover may lead you in new directions.

25. Go outside and lie on your back on the ground. Admire the clouds, birds, and nature with all its sounds and smells. Imagine your character doing the same thing in his or her setting and try to describe it from that character's point of view.

26. Just start writing—don't stress about the perfect words, sentence, or transitions. Write what ideas you do have; you can supplement and polish later.

## Verbal Brainstorming

If your usual brainstorming techniques aren't working for you, try verbal brainstorming, which was mentioned briefly above. I usually use this technique when I'm stuck or not sure if my ideas are strong enough. You'll need a trusted friend or writing partner for this. Start by reading all your notes on the project to your brainstorming partner. If you don't want to take that much time or go into that much depth, just describe the project for him, or limit the discussion to the particular area that's giving you trouble. Allow your brainstorming partner to ask questions and make suggestions as you discuss the issues that are concerning you. The simple process of explaining and discussing my ideas with a neutral third party almost always works out the kinks for me. Frequently, it also gives me leads into intriguing angles.

Brainstorm as much as you can both before you start a project and while you work on it. Brainstorming is what spurs you to start and continue outlining, what provides you with the inner resources to write with those magical elements infused in the most memorable books. Without it, the process would be dry—quite likely, you'd never make it past chapter three. Keep your ideas brewing fiercely from the start of each project right up until the day you write the words "The End" with a sigh of satisfaction and maybe even a tear in your eye.

*Now that you understand the importance of brainstorming throughout the 30-day method and while you're in the process of writing, it's time to start working on your preliminary outline.*

# CHAPTER 2

# Days 1–6:
# Your Preliminary Outline

In this chapter, you will create a preliminary outline, which will form the springboard for your story and the basis for a formatted outline. A preliminary outline consists of character and setting sketches, a research list, a plot sketch, a summary outline, miscellaneous scene notes, and closing scene notes. What you create during these six days will be incorporated into your formatted outline later, as you'll see in chapter five.

To create a preliminary outline, it's necessary to do some preparation. Obviously the very first thing you need to do is choose the story you're going to work on. In the previous chapter, we discussed the importance of constant brainstorming, as well as how essential it is to the creative process that you jot down notes about your ideas as they come to you and store them in individual project folders. When you're choosing a book to outline, ask yourself this question: Does it feel like this idea is ready to be transformed into a full outline? You can usually tell when a project is ready because you can't seem to exorcise it from your mind. Once you decide on an idea that's ready to go into outline form, get out your project folder for that book.

You'll be using Worksheets 1–7 in Appendix C to create your preliminary outline. You'll start with character, setting, and plot sketches, filling out your research list as you go. Once the basic sketches are fleshed out, you'll create a summary outline with the beginning scenes of the book, followed by miscellaneous and closing scene notes. Let's take a look at the day-by-day breakdown for Stage 1 of the 30-day method.

### Stage 1: Preliminary Outline

| Schedule | What to Complete |
|---|---|
| Day 1 | Character Sketches |
| Day 2 | Setting Sketches and Research List |
| Day 3 | Plot Sketch |
| Days 4–5 | Summary Outline |
| Day 6 | Miscellaneous Scene Notes and Closing Scene Notes |

Total: 6 days to a preliminary outline

As you work on the steps for the preliminary outline, keep in mind that it's a layering process. Your initial character sketches may be brief, but it's not the last you'll see of them. You'll be expanding on every step throughout every stage. Get down as much as you can during each step, trusting that the pieces will fall into place of their own accord eventually. To keep the story firmly fixed in your mind, go over what you've accomplished in these days often. This will encourage subsequent brainstorming, layering and strengthening of the story.

Also remember that these steps are for your own use. No one else will see this early work, so you don't have to worry about the quality of your writing. Don't worry about switching between past and present tense—none of that matters right now. The point is to get it down. The rich imagery, textured sentences, and clever turns of phrase all come later. The goal right now is to get started. Even if you're not sure whether you want to use an idea you have for the book, write it down.

Now let's get going.

## DAY 1: CHARACTER SKETCHES

Character sketches, like most aspects of outlining, are a process of brainstorming. When you flesh out character sketches for your story, write down everything that comes to you, no matter how trivial. Remember to give *all* your main characters (including the villain) internal and external conflicts. This will bring your characters to life.

When you first start using this outline system, you may find that you prefer to write your character sketches free-form instead of using a worksheet. When I first started outlining, I felt that in-depth character sketches developed from formatted worksheets focused on too many things unimportant to the immediate story. I eventually designed my own character sketch worksheet (Worksheet 1 in Appendix C), and I still use it for most of my novels. Feel free to use Worksheet 1 in the way most useful to you: You can fill it out as is, follow it loosely, or simply use it as a guideline for your own free-form character sketch.

In the brainstorming techniques listed on pages 12–14 of chapter one, I suggested you cut out pictures of people who resemble your characters from magazines. In the early years of my writing career I put together a special binder that I now find invaluable when brainstorming on a particular story. For each of my strongest novel ideas, I created a page that contains the book title along with the full names and magazine pictures of the main characters. I keep pictures of secondary characters, villains, and children of main characters in the back of the book.

If you can picture your characters clearly, actually *see* them, chances are you'll write about them in a more intimate, comfortable way—as if you know them well. That's what the character sketch worksheet is designed to help you do. It encourages you to think about your characters beyond just naming them. To get a better feel for the type of information that belongs in a character sketch, let's go over each section of the worksheet:

### Physical Descriptions

This section includes any—or all—of the following: a character's age, race, eye color, hair color and style, build (height/weight), skin tone, and style of dress (based on the time period and season of the year the book is set in). It can also include any other characteristics you deem important to the character or the book. If a character has any physical flaws, abnormalities, or disabilities, describe them and the affects they've had on his life and relationships.

You may wish to attach certain mannerisms to some of your characters to make them unique. Does your heroine have a habit of winding her hair around her finger when she's nervous? Does the hero rub the back of his neck when he's frustrated? Does a character have a particular phrase she uses often? In my novel *Forever Man*, the hero often used the phrase "six different ways to Sunday," and this habit began to define him and make him stand out from the other characters.

### Personality Traits

This is the section where you detail what kind of person your character is. Happy, somber, bookish, you name it. What are his strengths and weaknesses as a person? Does he have any vices? Hobbies? What kind of entertainment and food does he like? What are his least favorite forms of entertainment and food? What colors does he prefer? Be as detailed as you can because your outline and story will be stronger for it.

### Background

Just as people are shaped by their pasts, so too are characters. Background is very important in defining a character and making her three-dimensional. Creating a solid background for each main character will help you to fill out your entire outline in detail.

A main character backstory can include information on the character's parents, siblings, relatives, friends, old lovers, pets, life-shaping events and their long-term effects, etc. Did this character have a good home life during her childhood, a troubling one, or something in-between? What kind of schooling did she have? Was she popular, unpopular, in-between? What is her religion, if any? If she isn't religious, give some insight on this. Does she have a car preference? Does she drive fast or slow? Does she eat quickly or slowly? What are her feelings about alcohol, cigarettes, and drugs? Where did the character grow up? What is her ethnicity? How does this affect her? What does she consider some of her worst mistakes and greatest achievements? What goals does this character have? Has she done anything to achieve these goals? Why or why not?

When it comes to romantic and/or sexual relationships, what are the character's views on love? How does the opposite sex view her? How does the *same* sex view her? What are her preferences in a lover? Her sexual habits? Is she jealous or detached in a relationship? Why? Include all the information that comes to you.

### Internal Conflicts

All characters must have depth, and usually this comes from internal and external conflict. Internal conflict, or emotional turmoil, is usually handled with summary or narrative as a character reflects on his actions, judgments, and perceived mistakes. A solid, well-developed internal conflict or two makes characters more realistic and complex. Internal conflict also makes characters more interesting for readers because they are able to identify with a character's internal struggle to do what is right.

Be wary of having a main character whose purpose is limited to being the protector or "healer" of another main character. Each main character must have his own internal conflicts. I once wrote and rewrote one of my books, unable to figure out what the problem was—I just knew for a fact the book wasn't working. No matter what I did, it always fell flat. I sat in on a two-day workshop about characterization, and the speaker made me realize exactly what was wrong with my story: The hero in the book had absolutely no internal conflict. He was secretly in love with the heroine and trying to be her healer—that was his only motivation. He was a one-dimensional character who sparked no sympathy, understanding, or approval from the reader. At that point, all I needed to do to fix the book was create a character with his own problems.

### External Conflicts

External conflict is an outside or situational conflict that's preventing your main character from accomplishing his goal. Three well-known types of external conflict include man against man, man against society, and man against nature. Some examples include physical handicaps, an accident or loss that has scarred a main character physically or emotionally, or a relationship that eludes him or dominates his choices.

While I'm sure you can think of some genre stories that contain only external conflicts, the most effective plot is one that reveals both the inner and outer conflicts of your characters. Usually readers only root for characters they care about. Give them a good reason to sympathize.

### Occupation/Education

A character is defined by what he does (or doesn't) do for a living. Provide some insight into your character's chosen occupation and how he got there. For example, what educational requirements were necessary? What is this character's financial picture at the time the book takes place? How does this affect him? What is his level of intelligence, and what kind of influence has that had on his life and relationships? Don't worry about researching occupations at this point. Right now, just spend time on what his job is and why he does it. We'll get into researching specific occupations later.

### Miscellaneous Notes

You may want to further expand on the character by brainstorming on anything else that fleshes out the main characters in your mind.

If you're writing a paranormal or horror novel, there's less of a need to include personality traits or background information in your character sketch for the villain (who might be a vampire, demon, or some other creature that's not human). Readers don't have to understand a paranormal villain, because it's often simply the embodiment of evil. Therefore the reader is rightfully expected to feel nothing for the villain except fear, revulsion, and possibly helpless intrigue. There are exceptions. Anne Rice's creatures, for instance, are complex enough to warrant in-depth character sketches in the outline. If you feel yours are too, go ahead and flesh out your creatures with character sketches.

Now that we've gone over the sections of a character sketch worksheet, let's take a look at what a completed one would look like. On the next page, I created a character sketch for Susie Salmon, the main character in Alice Sebold's best-selling first novel, *The Lovely Bones*. Some areas weren't addressed in the book, so those fields are blank here. Since this will be the first worksheet you complete for your outline, you, too, may have some blank fields.

## CHARACTER SKETCH
## TITLE: *THE LOVELY BONES*

**Character Name:** Susie Salmon

**Nickname:**

**Birth Date/Place:**

**Character Role:** heroine

**PHYSICAL DESCRIPTIONS**

**Age:** 14 when murdered

**Race:** white

**Eye Color:** blue

**Hair Color/Style:** mousy brown

**Build (Height/Weight):**

**Skin Tone:**

**Style of Dress:** in life: bell-bottoms, mini skirts, and mini dresses, Danskin tights, vests

**Characteristics/ Mannerisms:**

**PERSONALITY TRAITS:**

**BACKGROUND:** In many ways, her family life was typical. A younger brother and sister. Family holidays with decorations and photos. Birthdays and Christmas. Memories.

She used to build model ships with her father. It was a bonding experience for both of them—something they always did together. They'd made dozens of the little ships over the years. He called her his "first mate."

She was closer in some ways to her father than to her mother. But she always wanted her mother's attention and approval. She liked being her mother's little girl.

She was playful with her little brother, Buckley. Piggyback rides.

**INTERNAL CONFLICTS:** Susie wants what she can't have. She wants to be allowed to grow up. She doesn't want to let go of her life on earth and she needs to watch her family and friends even after her death—wanting to rescue them from grief. In heaven, watching life continue on without her on the earth, she discovers that the dividing line between the living and the dead is sometimes blurry. Susie comes to believe that if she watches her family and friends closely and wants to badly enough, she might be able to change the lives of those she loves. She comes to believe that rescue from heaven, returning to her life on earth, is possible.

**EXTERNAL CONFLICTS:** Susie's killer is still free, and he wants to kill again. How can she prevent it from happening from her heaven? How can she keep her family together and strong in her absence?

**OCCUPATION/ EDUCATION:** 14-year-old in junior high school with aspirations to be a wildlife photographer or an Oscar-winning actress.

**MISCELLANEOUS NOTES:** Just starting to experience life, to notice boys. She has her first real crush.

At the end of Day 1, you should have gotten a good start on your character sketches. You'll be referring back to your character sketches often—adding new details and changing old ones whenever you feel the need—so be sure you keep them handy and leave yourself extra room. Don't worry about depth or organization right now. We'll go into more detail about those steps when we move on to Stage 4: Formatted Outline in chapter five.

## DAY 2: SETTING SKETCHES AND RESEARCH STRATEGIES

Once you have a firm idea of who your main characters are, it's time to start thinking about *where* they are. This is also the time to start planning the research you'll need to do in order to make your characters, setting, and entire story more realistic and specific.

### Setting Sketches

Before you start the story, you need to get to know your settings as well as your characters. Setting sketches, like character sketches, are very flexible. If all the characters live in the same area and time period, for example, you don't need to fill out this information for each character.

Worksheet 2A and Worksheet 2B in Appendix C will help you focus in on even the smallest details of a given setting. Worksheet 2A provides you with a guideline for creating a setting sketch for each general time period (year, season) and area (state, town). Worksheet 2B, on the other hand, provides you a guideline for creating a setting sketch for each character's owned or rented property (street, neighborhood, home, home interior, miscellaneous), as well as for his or her workplace setting.

These two worksheets may sound similar, but they're actually quite different in scope. Let's start by taking a closer look at Worksheet 2A, which focuses on the settings shared by several characters at the same time. You will need a separate worksheet for each city or town in your book. If the action takes place over several time periods or seasons, you may wind up with more than one sketch for each region. For instance, you may need a sketch of Juneau, Alaska, in both winter and spring. Now, let's look in detail at what this worksheet covers:

#### Name of Setting
It can be helpful to name each general setting by town and time period, especially if your book includes several settings or time periods.

#### Characters Living in Region/Time Period
List the characters who occupy this setting. This will help you keep track of who's living in your setting and when.

### Year or Time Period

The physical description of a setting depends very much on the time period in which your book is set. Detail as many specifics as you can in this area without doing significant research (that comes later).

### Season

In addition to the physical setting, the seasons in which your story takes place will determine the type of clothing your characters wear, along with the activities and transportation available to them.

### City and State

List any specifics you already know about the state and city hosting your story. At this point, you don't need to do extensive research for these fields—again, that comes later. Just include brief notes for each section.

### Miscellaneous Notes

This section will include any notes or details that would make the general setting clearer in your mind (and, therefore, in the reader's mind). For instance, is this setting undergoing a heat wave, a drought, unusually heavy snows?

This is also a good place to note how the location and time period affect the characters and the plot. How should the characters be dressed? Will the roads be dangerous or impassible in the winter? Do the characters need to watch out for flash floods?

Here's an example of a general setting sketch based on Elizabeth Dearl's mystery novel *Triple Threat.*

## GENERAL SETTING SKETCH
## TITLE: *TRIPLE THREAT*

**Name of Setting:** Perdue

**Characters Living in Region/Time Period:** Taylor Madison

**Year or Time Period:** Contemporary

**Season:** Winter

**City and State:** Perdue, Texas

**Miscellaneous Notes:** See corresponding Worksheet 2B for details.

Worksheet 2B, on the other hand, focuses on settings that are specific to certain characters, such as individual homes and offices. You will need to complete this worksheet for each of your main characters. If a character's home or workplace changes over the course of the book, make a new worksheet for the setting.

Again, don't worry about deep descriptions or about doing actual research on any of the locations you plan to use. That comes later. Right now, you just need to get the idea down. Just as you looked through magazines for pictures of people resembling your main characters, try looking through house magazines (*Traditional Home, Country Living, This Old House*, etc.) to find details on houses, rooms, furniture, and furnishings for a given story. Home renovation and decorating shows also can be great sources for inspiration.

I once read that a popular author pictures the same house for every one of her books. I'm the opposite. Most of my characters and settings come to me instinctively, and they're different for every book. My visions are extremely detailed, down to stairs, carpeting, furniture, types of wood, even plants. Maybe that comes from reading house magazines and watching renovation and decorating shows. If you're not picturing your settings in detail, look to magazines and television for inspiration.

In the meantime, Worksheet 2B will get you thinking in the right direction by forcing you to consider the following points:

### Character Name
Here, list the name of the character whose setting you're describing.

### General Settings to Include
Where does this character live or frequent? Does he own a home or rent a condo? Does he go to school? An office? Does he have a favorite spot by a river he likes to visit? Or a hiking trail he returns to when he needs to think? Look back to Worksheet 2A for inspiration.

### Character's Home Surroundings
You don't need extensive notes on the character's neighborhood, street, neighbors, etc., at this point. Jot down whatever thoughts you have, going into as much detail as you'd like without getting lost in research.

### Character's Workplace
Make notes about the character's workplace, just as you did with his home. If your character is in school, adapt the headings in this section according.

### Miscellaneous Notes
This is a good place to record additional thoughts or to indicate how your character feels about the general home and workplace settings.

Let's look at an example of a character setting sketch based on Taylor Madison, the heroine of Elizabeth Dearl's mystery novel *Triple Threat*.

## CHARACTER SETTING SKETCH
### TITLE: *TRIPLE THREAT*

**Character Name:** Taylor Madison

**GENERAL SETTINGS FOR THIS CHARACTER:** See corresponding Worksheet 2A for details.

**CHARACTER'S HOME SURROUNDINGS:**

**City or Town:** Perdue is a tiny West Texas town. It's clannish like most small towns. Outsiders aren't trusted; everyone knows everyone. Lots of scandals. A man's word still means a lot here. (See corresponding Worksheet 2A for more details.)

**Neighborhood:**

**Street:**

**Neighbors:** Busybody/gossip Dorothy

**Home:** a little house with scraggly rose bushes that she'd inherited when her father died

**Home Interior:** lots of odd items from garage sales, flea markets, and thrift shops

**CHARACTER'S WORKPLACE:** Taylor is a published author and an amateur sleuth.

**City or Town of Business:** See corresponding Worksheet 2A for details.

**Business Name:**

**Type of Business:**

**Neighborhood:**

**Street:**

**Individual Workspace:**

**Co-workers:**

**MISCELLANEOUS NOTES:**

As demonstrated in the example we just looked at, you may find that there are areas you aren't able to fill in just yet or details that you'd like to leave up in the air for the time being. That's perfectly fine. Just note what you can and remember that you can expand later. I'm often not able to fill in several areas in my setting sketches at first, but I set up the worksheet so I can drop new information into the sketch as soon as I come up with it. Here's an example from my paranormal romance, *Sweet Dreams*.

PARTIAL SETTING SKETCH
TITLE: *SWEET DREAMS*

**Home:** Cass lives on Hwy 54, in his parents' house (left to him after their deaths). The barn no longer holds animals, but his workshop. He owns _____ acres. Numerous types of trees surround the property. A clearing is located _____ feet from the house. Cass' special oak tree—The Protector—that once grew in this clearing is now a stump. Cass' house resembles a "deluxe" log cabin (two-story).

**Home Interior:** Inside, handmade furniture. Warm and cozy. High ceilings, exposed beams, clear-finished wood. Wood-burning fireplace in the center with a bear rug in front of it. Kitchen is exposed so that it and the living room, where the fireplace is located, is one huge room.

## Research List

If you haven't started researching your idea already, the preliminary outline phase is the time to start. Use Worksheet 3 in Appendix C to create a list of topics that you know you're going to need to research. Please note that this research list is *not* the place for actual research. It's merely a list of what you think you'll need to research later.

For instance, you may need to research your characters' careers so you've got a clear idea of what's done and why, overall and day-to-day. You may need to interview people in a certain profession or area of expertise, or research the places your characters live in or travel to. You may need to research clothing, etc., for the time period your book is set in. If you're writing a book set in colonial times, for example, you'll need to research the types of clothing worn by men, women, and children during that time, in all social classes and parts of the country. If a character has a medical condition or develops one during the course of the book, you'll need to research that. If your book is a mystery or suspense novel, you may need to research police procedures or specific agencies, such as a local police department (in a small town or big city), the FBI, or the CIA. You may need to research specific trees or animals indigenous to an area, historical events, or laws—particularly state laws, as they may differ greatly from federal. If you don't feel you have enough knowledge of a subject to write about it easily, that subject needs to go on your research list.

Write down anything that you're going to need to research for the book—big or small. The research list doesn't need to be typed.

Let's take a look at an example of completed research list using *Girl With a Pearl Earring*, Tracy Chevalier's historical novel, as a model.

## RESEARCH LIST
### TITLE: *GIRL WITH A PEARL EARRING*

1. The artist Johannes Vermeer (1632–1675), including his body of work (specific paintings), life, family, home and his studio within it, friends, and fans of his paintings.
2. Clothing styles in the time period the book is set in (1664–1676), specific to the setting and social classes.
3. Settings and weather conditions in the Netherlands—including Delft, the Oude Lagendijck, Molenpoort, Papists' Corner, Rielveld Canal, Schie River, etc.—in the time period.
4. Religion (Protestant and Catholic) in this time period and setting.
5. Guild of St. Luke.
6. Careers and social hierarchies of the time period and setting for: tile making and apprenticeships of the trade, servants, painters, traders, butchers, soldiers, apothecaries, etc.
7. Home furnishings, food, money—specific to the time period and setting.
8. The process of painting specific to the time period and setting, including but not limited to lighting, shadows, colors, materials, and the methods of preparing and storing the materials necessary for painting.
9. The camera obscura—specific to the time period and setting.
10. The plague in this time period and setting.
11. Childbirth and sexual mores in this time period and setting.

If you have time when you finish the outline for the project you're doing now, start filling out the research list for each of the books you have in project folders. This will become your "shopping list." If you work things efficiently, you can start doing research between projects, well in advance of beginning a book. We'll talk more about this in chapter three.

Since your research list should be fairly easy to fill out, you should be to get it almost completed as you're working on your setting sketches on Day 2 of the schedule.

# DAY 3: PLOT SKETCHES

Like a tapestry, every story is woven of threads that become invisible within the overall design. By familiarizing yourself with story threads and being aware of them as you read, you can learn to weave story threads skillfully into your own novel.

## Understanding Story Threads

Identifying story threads and mentally following them throughout the outline reduces the need for multiple revisions and will certainly make you a more productive writer. For outlining purposes, we'll look at threads beyond the traditional scope of individual plot and subplot threads. Instead, we'll also be looking at individual tension threads, release threads, etc. All of these threads work together to form your plot sketch. With this in mind, your outline will consist of the following seven to eight threads (nine or ten for a romance novel):

- story goal (or theme)
- romance thread (optional, depending on genre)
- subplot threads
- plot tension
- romantic/sexual tension (optional, depending on genre)
- release
- downtime
- black moment (or climax)
- resolution
- aftereffects of resolution (optional)

Your plot sketch is your first real opportunity to start thinking about and developing each one of the threads listed above. Worksheet 4 in Appendix C takes you through each thread individually and provides you with prompts to get the ideas rolling. You can revise this worksheet often. It will be especially helpful to you when your formatted outline is complete.

We'll discuss most of the plot threads in greater detail in chapter four when we go over Stage 3: Story Evolution. Remember, at this stage you probably won't be able to fill in all of these sections, but it's still important to start thinking about them. Simply write in whatever you can for each section and remember you can go back and add more later. Let's explore each thread.

## Story Goal

A story goal is the central idea of a novel. You will relate it to your readers through the plot, major conflict, and character interactions. In all genres of fiction, the story goal is the catalyst of the book—the reason why the characters are there, the reason why the story evolves, the reason why the reader opens the book, starts and keeps reading. All other threads and characters are involved in achieving the story goal.

In some books, the story goal seems more like the theme in that the main characters are not striving to accomplish any single major goal and there is no clear-cut course of action. Instead, such books rely on overarching central concepts that are represented through the plot and characters. (You'll notice this in *The Lovely Bones* example we'll look at shortly). However, in most books, especially commercial fiction, there is a clear-cut story goal that can be identified and charted throughout the course of the story. If you don't feel your book has a clear-cut story goal, substitute the word "Theme" for this field and continue.

It's important that you identify the major conflict or main theme of your book before continuing as this will affect your entire story. What are all the characters assembled and striving for? Write as much as you can on this important thread. You'll be going back over it and tweaking it often to fit your changing concepts of the book, so don't worry if you come up with very little right now. Even one sentence is enough to begin with. Chapter four will help you work out any kinks in the evolution of your story goal.

Let's take a look at some story goal examples:

- In *Fear Nothing* by Dean Koontz, Christopher Snow has a very rare genetic disorder that leaves him dangerously vulnerable to light. In an attempt to save his life, his scientist mother comes up with a revolutionary new approach to the engineering of retroviruses. Unfortunately, the experiment has gone horribly wrong, and Christopher discovers it and begins to piece together the puzzle of what has now put the world at risk of contamination.
- A wealthy American is found stabbed multiple times in the night compartment of the Calais coach in Agatha Christie's classic *Murder on the Orient Express.* By morning, every traveler on board has become a suspect with a secret. Good thing the ingenious Hercule Poirot is on board to solve the crime.

## Romance Thread (Optional)

In a romance novel, the most important part of the book is the relationship between the hero and the heroine. This long-term thread is as important as the story goal, and it continues from the beginning of the story until it ties up with the happily-ever-after theme. It should be in every, or almost every, scene of the book, and should be woven in seamlessly with all other plot threads. Anything that happens affects the romance, just as the romance will have influence over the other plot aspects.

When you're using romance as a long-term thread, you want to keep it foremost in your mind, which is why it has its own section on the plot sketch worksheet. In genres outside romance, this thread is a subplot since it's not the dominating aspect of the plot. If you include a minor subplot of romance in your novel, remember that this thread needs a beginning, middle, and satisfactory resolution just as all other threads do. If your book isn't a romance or doesn't include a long-term romance thread, you don't need to do anything with this section on the plot sketch worksheet.

Take a look at these romance thread examples:

- In the young-adult romance *Waiting Games* by Bruce and Carole Hart, fourteen-year-old Jessie is in love with her nineteen-year-old guitar teacher, Michael. The differences in their ages may prove to be more than a little complication in this growing-up-too-fast love story.

- Is it a blessing or a curse when Catherine Earnshaw's father finds the homeless Heathcliff as a young boy and brings him home to live with the family? In Emily Brontë's *Wuthering Heights*, Heathcliff and Catherine's relationship is wild, passionate, tumultuous, and tormented—to the grave.

## Subplot Threads

Subplots function as secondary plots. They typically contrast or run parallel to the main plot. They can also function outside the realm of the main plot, existing largely to provide a change of scene, emotion, or tone. These threads should work in harmony to effectively develop both character and plot. Each will depend on the others as the novel comes to a close.

Subplots can range from health conditions and financial worries to physical or mental conclusions a character must reach: returning home after a family member dies, moving out of an apartment, changing careers. In all cases, it should be clear to readers how the subplots connect with the main story goal.

How many of these subplot threads you include depends on the length and complexity of your novel. There is no standard number. I've found that books with more than 60,000 words generally end up with at least eight subplot threads. Books closer to 100,000 words may end up with a few more. The more main characters and conflicts you have, the more subplot threads you'll end up with. Remember that you will have to give regular attention to all of your subplots. Even with a complex plot line, you never want to leave *any* of your threads for too long. You want to create tension, not forgetfulness and frustration in the reader. (We'll go into more detail about subplot threads in later chapters.)

At times, events in your story will cause some of your subplot threads to merge. This is perfectly acceptable. In fact, in some ways it's desirable. You want your threads to mesh to the point that you've created a net your characters won't easily find their way out of. If your characters can't see a way out, neither will your reader.

The subplot section on your plot sketch worksheet may prove to be the hardest for you to fill out simply because most stories have several subplots working together with the story goal. For now, write what comes to you, even if it's only a few words under each subplot number. Don't worry about putting the threads in order of importance.

Here are a few subplot thread examples:

- Mara Jade was a dancer at Jabba the Hutt's palace the day Luke Skywalker came to rescue Han Solo. Mara's true master was the Emperor, and she was sent to kill

Luke that day. In *Heir to the Empire*, the first book in Timothy Zahn's masterful Star Wars trilogy, Mara believes Luke killed her master, and she wants revenge. The main plot of this book focuses on the resurrection of the Imperial fleet, preparing to strike back at the Rebel Alliance.

- In the children's book *The Bad Beginning (A Series of Unfortunate Events)* by Lemony Snicket, twelve-year-old Klaus Baudelaire loves books. After his parents are killed in a fire, Klaus and his two sisters are sent to live with Count Olaf, a perfectly horrible situation and the main plot. The children only find solace in their neighbor, Justice Strauss, who has a library full of books—books that may help the Baudelaire children legally save themselves.

## Plot Tension

In all genres, plot tension is essential. This kind of tension is anything that brings the reader to a fever pitch of anticipation. A story without plot tension leaves the reader uninvolved and unemotional.

Plot tension is extremely tricky to achieve and sustain. You need to bring readers to the snapping point and only then give them what they want—*temporarily*. You can tease the reader by snatching a resolution away just as it seems the tension is about to break, but don't do this too often. If you grab resolution out of the reader's hands too many times, you may lose him. On the other hand, if you give him what he wants too soon, you take away his motivation to keep reading.

Take a look at these examples of plot tension:

- *The Sword of Shannara* by Terry Brooks pits all of mankind against the Warlock Lord. Seeking the Sword of Shannara, mankind's only hope for survival against the evil confronting them, the companions Hendel, Menion, Balinor, Dayel, and Durin reach the tower of the Druids' Keep. The sword is theirs! As they enter the rounded chamber and stare in awe at the treasure, the display begins to dissolve in front of their eyes. They realize it was a trap. Before they can react, a huge rock slab shuts them into an inescapable prison.
- Summer McAfee is the owner of the Daisy Fresh cleaning service in Karen Robards's *Walking After Midnight*. She's cleaning the mortuary at 2 A.M. She's exhausted and her mind is working overtime because of the dead bodies in the room with her. Telling herself there's only one way to reassure herself that one of the bodies hadn't moved, she reaches out to touch it. Her hand is suddenly in the grip of—not a corpse!—a man very much alive. I won't give it all away here, but needless to say tension can't be far behind in a setup like this.

## Romantic/Sexual Tension (Optional)

In a romance novel, romantic/sexual tension is essential. You want to start this tension as early in the story as you possibly can. If you don't start the suspense promptly and keep it intense, the reader will be disappointed—or worse, embarrassed—during moments she should be temporarily relieved or exalted.

If you want to include a romance subplot in a genre outside of romance, you may choose to do so very subtly or more intensely, depending on how important the romance is within your story.

The examples below show romantic/sexual tension in subtle and relatively blatant forms:

- In Tracy Chevalier's *The Lady and the Unicorn*, Nicolas des Innocents is commissioned to design six lavish tapestries for Jean Le Viste, a French nobleman. Nicolas is a playboy to the extreme, a hunter and seducer of every woman, regardless of social class. Nicolas even attempts to seduce Le Viste's own daughter, Claude, by telling her the tale of the unicorn with his horn of special power that makes all pure again. Naturally, flirtatious sexual tension ensues between Nicolas and Claude.
- In Tracy Morgan's no-holds-barred category romance, *Michael's Wife*, the backstory reveals that Michael died while being held hostage with his best friend, Sloan, who managed to survive. During their captivity, Michael talked endlessly about his wife, Jesse, and even showed Sloan pictures of her. As a result, Sloan fell in love with the woman. In fact, dreaming about making love to her actually helped Sloan survive the ordeal. Though Michael's death wasn't easy for Jesse, as time passes, she begins to fantasize constantly about a dark lover coming to her—one who resembles the photos of Michael's friend Sloan. And so the stage is set for a rich and tense romance.

## Release

A release is an easement of plot or romantic tension. In a mystery, a release might take the form of a resolution of one aspect of the main problem. In a romantic or sexual thread or subplot, a release could be a kiss, lovemaking, or a declaration of feelings. The final words in a story should also produce a release that satisfies the readers and makes them long to revisit the story again, even if only in their minds.

Here are some examples of release:

- In *The Princess Bride* by William Goldman, three criminals kidnap Buttercup, the prince's future wife. The four of them have been followed every step of the way by the Dread Pirate Roberts. However, Buttercup has realized that the pirate is in fact her beloved Westley. Westley rescues Buttercup and they rush away from her captors, straight into the Fire Swamp. As they're making their way through snow sand and bursts of flame, Westley tells Buttercup how he became the Dread Pirate Roberts and made his fortune so he could return to his autumn-haired love. While the action is intense as Westley reveals his pirating adventures, there's an easement in the plot tension as he tells his tale.

- In Colleen McCullough's *The Thorn Birds*, Meggie escapes from her intolerable marriage and lives for a stolen moment she's longed for all her life with the handsome and ambitious priest Ralph de Briscassart. Finally, the one man she truly loves actually loves her back.

## Downtime

Downtime is a form of release, but it happens during a time of incredible tension. It should be one of the most poignant scenes in your novel. During downtime, which comes at the end of the middle section of the book, the main character may step back from the action and reflect on what happily-ever-after could have been (if not for all the obstacles you put in his way). For a time, the main character also may believe that the story goal is unachievable, and he may seem to give up the fight.

The reader is led to an even higher level of anticipation because of downtime. In a romance, this is a glimpse of the hero and heroine living happily ever after—a sensual or emotional scene, or a stolen moment in a chaotic time. In any other genre, downtime is a temporary respite from the extreme tension the plot is creating—a bittersweet moment of some sort.

Following downtime, your character will again realize that he must act, and he'll find a new way to attempt resolution. Never for one moment, however, will the main character feel a sense of satisfaction or contentedness about this new course of action—he must be utterly tormented at every turn. This new plan of action will be his final, desperate attempt to reach the story goal, and the ground won't feel at all solid as he moves forward. In some cases, your character will come to the decision to act because the stakes of the conflict are again raised—danger is near, and he must move forward whether he wants to or not. This episode will provide the motivation to propel the story to the next level.

In nearly every situation, downtime must be followed with a black moment. Downtime releases the tension for a short period, and that tension must be built back up quickly or you risk losing your reader.

Here are some examples of the calm before the storm with downtime:

- Edward is a neuroscientist in *Acceptable Risk* by Robin Cook. He and Kim have just moved in together, but the arrangement has been anything but ideal. His new designer-drug research has taken over his entire life, to the point where he and his team of researchers are actually taking this experimental new drug themselves. He apologizes to Kim out of the blue and takes her to dinner. He tells her all about the progress they've made with the drug Ultra. The drug makes them feel relaxed, focused, confident, and content. It's enhanced their long-term memory and alleviated fatigue, anger, and anxiety. It's an absolutely perfect drug for the socially awkward. Kim is happy that Edward seems to be with her again . . . until he insists that she take Ultra, too.

- In H.G. Wells's *The Island of Dr. Moreau*, the beast people have killed their creator, the evil genius Dr. Moreau. The Law is gone, and the unnatural abominations Moreau tormented in the name of science and discovery now have a taste for blood and revenge. As the humans Prendick and Montgomery lock themselves in the compound, Prendick realizes there is no way off the island.

## Black Moment

The black moment in the story is commonly referred to as the climax of the book. The worst of all horrors is happening or has happened, and the main characters (as well as the readers) are now thoroughly convinced the future will never be happy. The black moment, which occurs in the first part of the end section of the book (when tension is at its highest), leaves the reader and the characters wondering whether evil will overcome good.

If you're writing a romance novel, you'll have two black moments—one black moment for the story goal and one for the romance thread. The black moment for the romance thread usually occurs in the end section of the book, just after the story goal has been resolved satisfactorily. Most genres have only one black moment for the story goal.

You can see that the black moment has arrived in these examples:

- In *Relic* by Douglas Preston and Lincoln Child, a creature has murdered unsuspecting patrons in the New York Museum of Natural History and taken out a heavily armed SWAT team. FBI agent Pendergast has trapped it and shot it repeatedly. Yet moments later, Pendergast hears shooting in the hall. The creature is still alive. Is it possible to kill it?
- In Greg Iles's *24 Hours*, Hickey's mother is dead, and Hickey believes that her doctor, Will, killed her. Hickey seeks revenge against Will by breaking into the house of Will's wife, Karen, and kidnapping their daughter. Although Hickey promises Karen no one will be killed if he gets the financial restitution he wants, things go downhill. He asks Karen, hypothetically, who she'd rather he kill—her daughter or herself? Karen realizes that the question is anything but hypothetical. If she doesn't do something now, Hickey will kill one or both of them, the only question is when.

## Resolution

The resolution, or denouement, of a story, comes after the climax when the story's main problems have been resolved. This is your chance to tie up any loose ends and provide satisfying conclusions for your subplot threads. The resolutions for the long-term story threads (story goal and, in romances, the romance thread) should be relatively clean, but subplot thread resolutions may not tie up quite so neatly (e.g., death or some other legitimate dead end). Tying up these loose ends is crucial to leaving the reader satisfied. I don't mean you have to provide a happy ending. A satisfactory resolution doesn't allow the reader to wonder about dangling plot threads or to feel cheated—you, as the writer, must fulfill the underlying promise of a logical, acceptable conclusion, even if it isn't a happy one.

Here are some stories that leave the reader satisfied without a happily-ever-after:

- In Alice Sebold's novel *The Lovely Bones*, you, as the reader, desperately want all wrongs to be righted for the main character, Suzie. In many ways, that's achieved during the course of the story, yet realistically there's no way for Suzie to get all she deserves. There isn't really a happily-ever-after in this story, but you're satisfied with the conclusion, and you accept the resolution.

- In the novel *The Tommyknockers* by Stephen King, the hero, Gard, sacrifices his life to save the town and the woman he loves. As a reader, you're devastated because you've come to care about Gard and believe he deserves to be happy after all he's been through, yet realistically you know there was nothing else he could do to remain a hero in your eyes. You accept the resolution because it's the only logical choice, and you're satisfied.

## Aftereffects of Resolution (Optional)

An aftereffect of a resolution may come in the form of an emotional reaction or an event that carries a story goal or subplot thread beyond its conclusion. In other words, the thread may continue even after it's been resolved.

Very few writers include aftereffects of resolution, though they're used frequently in movies. The novels discussed below used aftereffects of resolution in the form of twist endings:

- In Michael Crichton's magnificent *Sphere*, a strange sphere that gives the extraordinary, horrific power of being able to turn thoughts into reality is found at the bottom of the ocean. The three survivors of the chaos that follows the sphere's discovery retain this awesome power even after the sphere is destroyed. They realize that together they can "forget" this knowledge by thinking their forgetfulness of it into reality. I don't want to completely ruin the beauty of this ending for those who haven't read the book, but let's just say that one of the survivors doesn't want to part with the newfound gift.

- In *Presumed Innocent* by Scott Turow, a twist ending completely takes the unsuspecting reader by surprise. While Rusty Sabich is found not guilty on charges of killing a former lover, the reader is never entirely certain throughout the book that he didn't do it. He had motive, opportunity, and the evidence pointed to him. In fact, you can't help but believe he did it and got away with it. Following his exoneration, Rusty is working in the yard and finds a clawed crowbar with blood and hair on it—clearly the murder weapon. He starts to wash it clean. Again, I hate to ruin this incredible surprise for those who haven't read it, but the murderer—someone whom you'd never have suspected—appears, and suddenly it all makes sense.

## Weaving Threads Into Your Plot Sketch

As you're puzzling out your outline, keep all your plot threads in mind—they'll come up again and again. Once you've added detail and depth to your outline and developed your story, the threads should become almost invisible. They'll become wonderfully cohesive and solid. Without foundation, your story would either melt into an unrecognizable puddle on the floor or fall flat on its face, unable to stand. With a cohesive structure, your story can breathe, walk, talk, and *live* all by itself.

Go into as much detail as possible on your plot sketch, but keep in mind that your first pass will be light on details. Don't worry. Over the next twenty-seven days, it will grow significantly.

Let's again look at *The Lovely Bones* for an example of what a completed plot sketch might look like:

PLOT SKETCH
TITLE: *THE LOVELY BONES*

**Story Goal:** After fourteen-year-old Susie is murdered by a neighbor, she watches from her heaven as her family, friends, and murderer live out their lives. She watches with envy and sadness as she's unable to return to them and live out her own life.

**Romance Thread (Optional):**

**Subplot Threads:**
1. Hyper-aware of the movements of his son, wife, and remaining daughter, Susie's father tries to ensnare her killer.
2. Susie's sister Lindsey hardening herself to stay strong.

4
WORKSHEET

3. Ray Singh, the boy who'd loved her, moving on with his life. The relationship between Susie Salmon and Ray Singh, before and after Susie's death, is secondary to the main plot.

4. Ruth Connors's obsession with Susie; Ruth's gift of sight—one that leads to a miracle.

5. Heaven, where Susie walks the paths to find what she needs but when she walks too far, she lives the perpetual yesterday of her death again. Because she can't give up on her life on earth, there is no joy in her heaven.

6. Susie's mother trying "to find a doorway out of her ruined heart."

7. Susie's young brother, always protected, believing that those who go away always come back.

**Plot Tension:** Overarching plot tension continues as Susie is unable to move on in her afterlife—she can't stop watching as the lives of her family and friends unfold, and she longs for all that she's missing out on. Additional long-term plot tension comes from the people Susie left behind, including her killer, as they struggle to continue with their lives.

**Romantic/Sexual Tension:** The tender first love between Susie and Ray, in life and in death.

**Release:** There's a temporary easement of tension when Susie's family learns for certain that she has been murdered and will never be coming home. The waiting and wondering ceases, and the grieving begins.

**Downtime:** Small, quick glimpse of what happily-ever-after would be for Susie and her family and friends if not for the obstacles standing in the way.

**Black Moment:** Readers are led to believe happily-ever-after may never be attained for Susie and her family and friends because the obstacles now appear monumental. Black moments include the separation of Susie's parents, and the desire of Susie's killer to strike again, possibly killing Susie's sister.

**Resolution:** A satisfying conclusion is reached for Susie and her family and friends as long- and short-term plot threads are resolved. Susie's parents reunite, her sister marries and has a child, Susie finally lets go of her loved ones, etc.

**Aftereffects of Resolution (optional):**

At the end of Day 3 in your schedule, you should have completed a very basic plot sketch of your book. Make a hard copy and go over it as often as you work in order to add layers of complexity to your story.

## DAYS 4–5: THE SUMMARY OUTLINE

During Days 4 and 5 of the 30-day method, you'll start writing your preliminary outline in the form of a summary essay, describing the images and specific details you already have in mind. (Worksheet 5 in Appendix C should get you started.)

Summarizing a story as you're preparing a preliminary outline will put the story's central elements firmly in your mind. Things will begin to collate in a stronger way. The story will be on the page now because of your outlining, but more importantly, it's firmly fixed in your head, where you can arrange, rearrange, and work with it. (You can do the same within your outline.) You should use any of the information you've already come up with in your character, setting, and plot sketches as you work.

In essence, your summary outline details the opening scene of your book and moves forward scene by scene through the story. For now, try to cover the beginning of the book in a linear (chronological) fashion without worrying about the middle or end scenes of the book. Day 6 will cover miscellaneous (nonlinear) scene notes and closing scene notes.

Let's look at a sample summary inspired by Dennis Lehane's best-selling novel, *Mystic River*.

### SUMMARY OUTLINE
### TITLE: *MYSTIC RIVER*

Starting in 1975, how Sean Devine, Jimmy Marcus, and Dave Boyle became friends. Sean's and Jimmy's fathers worked at Coleman Candy plant. Dave lives near Jimmy. They live in East Buckingham. Sean is from "the Point," which is "working class, blue collar, Chevys and Fords and Dodges parked in front of simple A-frames and the occasional small Victorian." In the Point, people own their homes. In the Flats, where Jimmy and Dave live, people rent. Sean goes to school at Saint Mike's Parochial in suits and ties. Jimmy and Dave go to Lewis M. Dewey School in street clothes. If not for their fathers, they might not have been friends.

A memory of the time Jimmy jumped down on the tracks at South Station to get their errant hockey ball. People on the platform went nuts. At the last moment, Jimmy was pulled up by several people. Jimmy isn't bothered by any of this, but Dave throws up in his own hands and Sean looks away.

Sean's father later tells him he can't play at Jimmy's house anymore. He has to stay in view of his own house. Jimmy is simply too wild, making him a bad influence on Sean.

In most cases, you'll be able to brainstorm enough to fill a few single-spaced pages of your summary. You can probably already visualize what the first scenes of *Mystic River* look like since there's a steady progression from paragraph to paragraph, but don't feel that your summary outline has to be entirely cohesive. You may realize as you're writing that you're not sure what the next scene really needs to include. It's fine to write yourself a note within your summary outline—"Scene here?"—and then move on with the story.

At the end of Day 5, you should have a fairly good start on the beginning of your outline. Remember to keep adding to your research list as needed, and go over what you've accomplished often to keep the story fixed in your mind and to encourage new brainstorming, layering, and strengthening of the story.

## DAY 6: MISCELLANEOUS SCENE NOTES AND CLOSING SCENE NOTES

Inevitably, as you're working on a brand new story, you're going to hit a snag in the summary outline where you don't know what should happen for many scenes in a row. Yet you still have additional ideas about what will happen later. That's where miscellaneous scene notes and closing scene notes come into play.

### Miscellaneous Scene Notes

Worksheet 6 in Appendix C, miscellaneous scene notes, is for anything that doesn't fit into the outline just yet but still relates to the beginning or middle of your story. These notes could be about elements or threads you're unsure of or vague ideas you want to remember to explore later. Write everything free-form.

At this stage, every story sounds a little strange or disjointed. Readers won't have the benefit of your vision, so it's best not to seek the opinion of many (or any) outside readers for a preliminary outline. As chaotic and unattached as miscellaneous scene notes seem on paper, however, writing down such information is vital because it widens your perspective. You want to have these notes and ideas available when the time comes to insert them precisely where they need to be in the formatted outline.

Using *Tom Clancy's Op-Center* as our inspiration, let's look at an example of miscellaneous scene notes detailing what some of the author's early thoughts on scenes to come might have looked like:

MISCELLANEOUS SCENE NOTES
TITLE: *TOM CLANCY'S OP-CENTER*

The Op-Center computer and all places (including CIA and Defense, etc.) that Op-Center supplies data to go down for twenty seconds—an impossibility because of the way the system is set up.

Op-Center discovers from NRO photos that North Korea is deploying brigades south from the capital with a perimeter around the Southern Hemisphere. War seems inevitable.

## Closing Scene Notes

Closing scene notes relate specifically to your book's final scenes. Since, at this early stage, you may not know exactly how everything will come together at the end of your story, notes in this section will be fairly general and nonlinear. Odds are, they won't even fit into your outline in a chronological order just yet. Because you'll want to remember them in as much detail as possible so that you'll be able to drop them into the outline exactly where they're needed later, it's crucial that you write them down now anyway. Write them free-form using Worksheet 7 in Appendix C. Include closing scene notes in the same document as your summary outline and miscellaneous scene notes.

Closing scenes are very important to building the structure of your outline, and eventually, your novel. The more pieces we can create for your story now, the easier it will be to put them together in the right order when it's time.

Here's an example of closing scene notes based on *Where the Red Fern Grows* by Wilson Rawls:

CLOSING SCENE NOTES
TITLE: *WHERE THE RED FERN GROWS*

During the end chapters, Billy goes hunting in Cyclone Timber Country. Old Dan and Little Ann (his coon dogs) tree a mountain lion—the devil cat of the Ozarks. After a terrible fight, the mountain lion is killed. Little Ann is wounded. Old Dan is eviscerated. Though Billy's mom sews him up, Old Dan dies. Not long afterward, the life goes out of Little Ann without her brother, and she dies, too.

At the end of Day 6, you'll have miscellaneous scene notes and closing scene notes for your book. Keep everything in a working project folder. If you have a question about something while you're working, you don't want to have to go on an all-out search to find the answer. Having everything together will keep you organized. Go back over everything you've accomplished often, layering and strengthening where you can, brainstorming continuously.

*Look how much you've accomplished in a mere six days! You've built a strong foundation for what's to come. We still have a few steps to go before the preliminary outline can be used to create a formatted (final) outline. With all the seeds of a healthy preliminary outline planted and steadily growing, we're ready to move on to researching your book.*

# CHAPTER 3

# Days 7–13: Researching Your Idea

Research is necessary for any writer. For some, it's a necessary *evil*. Because of my dislike of research, I developed a system to make it much more palatable for each project. Incidentally, it's also much more efficient in the scheme of my career. Most writers know *why* they have to research and *how* to do it. It's really the *when* of it that's a stumbling block.

In this chapter, we're going to talk about when to research for your books and how to approach research while keeping your outline in mind. We'll also discuss some crucial outline aids designed to help you prepare for later stages of the outlining process.

### Stage 2. Research

| Schedule | What to Complete |
|---|---|
| Days 7–13 | Research your book and complete any outline aid worksheets you need. |

Total: 7 days to completed research

The schedule provides seven days to complete any research and outline aid worksheets you need for your novel. Please note there is no day-to-day breakdown of the schedule for this stage. Research is very involved; you'll find your own efficient way to accomplish what you need. However, I will be providing tips to help maximize your productivity throughout this stage.

Does completing all your research in seven days sound impossible? It may well be the first few times you use this method, especially for authors who generally spend nine months out of every given year researching, and for those authors with extremely complex plots. In order to get to the point where your research requires only a week in the outline process, you'll need to get the whole of your writing career in order. We'll talk more about getting ahead of your manuscript submissions or book releases in chapter ten. If the pace becomes too much for you, simply slow down (flexibility is the beautiful thing about this method). Take the time you need to research your story, then come back to the schedule when you're ready to move forward.

# WHEN TO RESEARCH

Ideally, you will learn to make the most of your research time by planning it far in advance and getting started on it long before you begin a specific project. As we discussed earlier, it's essential to have many stories brewing at the same time. You won't be able to write them all at once, but you *will* be able to start gathering your research materials well in advance of working on each project. As you create project folders for the most promising stories in your creative coffeepot, make sure you include a blank research list (Worksheet 3 in Appendix C) in each one. Get started writing down the types of things you might have to research for the individual projects, creating something like grocery lists for yourself.

Weeks, months, even years before I begin work on any of the fifty-plus ideas brewing in my creative coffeepot, I start scoping out books and other materials for that story. If you're not haunting used bookstores, flea markets, and annual library or school book sales, now is the time to start. Traditional bookstores, virtual bookstores, and book clubs will also be invaluable to you. I have tons of books on my shelves that I bought specifically for a project that I haven't yet started.

This is also the time to start gathering contacts—experts you might need to interview somewhere down the road. Police officers, private detectives, doctors, lawyers, etc., can prove to be very helpful when you need specific information only they can provide. Start meeting and getting to know some of the professionals who will be able to help you with the details of your research later.

Why start gathering your research for a project so far in advance? To give yourself time to do the bulk of your research *between projects*. We will discuss setting goals that allow you to get ahead of your manuscript submissions and book releases and you'll create an annual goal sheet, which will cover everything you'll do that year. Even when you're not actively writing anything, you can still do research. In fact, doing your research when you're not worried about impending deadlines is ideal, since there will be less stress and more time for you to focus on the tasks at hand.

It's up to you whether to make notes with a pen and paper or to actually type your notes as you research. I recommend using a highlighter, pen, and a pad of paper (less work and less stress). Then, during the seven scheduled days for research when you're outlining, you can type up your research notes and create reference sheets for easy access to the research you need. Doing it this way will refresh your mind on everything you learned while you were doing the research.

Another great way to make the most of your research time is to consolidate your research. If you write in a genre like mystery or horror, the research you do can be used for many projects. I write a police procedural series with a partner. We recycle a lot of the research we do on police work from book to book in the series, and I've carefully created and maintained binders that keep the massive amounts of research we do as organized as possible. Any time I need a fact about some aspect of police work, I can flip open this binder to the precise section that will help me find my answer. Any additional research we do for each book in the series is generally focused on something particular about that plot, such as specific crimes (armed robbery or strangling, for instance).

## WHY RESEARCH IN THE OUTLINE STAGE

It's best to do your major research *before* you begin your formatted outline in Step 4 of the 30-day method. Research often reveals important details and facts that affect your entire story. Building a strong foundation before you get in too deep allows you to develop a clearer and more complex concept of your story. Ultimately, researching early in the outlining process saves you time later, during the revision process.

For my novel *Reluctant Hearts*, I waited until I had completed my outline to start my research. I literally waited until the last minute, so I ended up doing all my research in a single weekend. The research I did changed my outline considerably, especially from the middle to the end. I planned to start writing on Monday, so I not only had to complete all my research during that one weekend, I also had to scramble to incorporate all I'd learned into the outline. Scenes needed to be created, expanded, altered, or deleted altogether. Had I waited to do the research until after I started writing the book itself, I would have had to interrupt a couple days of writing, as well disrupt my annual goal sheet, in order to get everything straight. By researching before you begin outlining, you can avoid making this mistake and save yourself time later.

The point is, it's very hard to write a story with huge holes in your own knowledge. It's essentially doing the work backwards and creating a considerable amount of extra work for yourself in the process. Not very productive.

Of course, situations will arise when you realize, after completing the outline or while you're writing the book, that you need to do additional research. If it's minor—and in some cases, even if it's major—you can do the research while you're writing or after you finish the book. Simply incorporate the research into the book as you edit and polish the first draft. We'll discuss this in more detail in chapter nine.

As a rule, do your research before or during outlining. However, exceptions to this rule do exist. There are certain types of research for mystery novels or other complex genres that should be done only when the formatted outline is almost finished. For instance, if you need to interview a police detective for your novel, you may not know exactly what to ask until the outline is nearly complete. Unless you're very good friends with the police officer or detective you need to interview, you will annoy him if you call with every little question as it comes up. Wait until your outline is pretty well done so you only have to interview him once.

In a situation like this, it helps to keep a running list of all the questions you need to ask this person during the interview. You can use Worksheet 8 in Appendix C for this purpose. Begin this list as soon you start to research your story, and keep it in your project folder so you can tweak it whenever you need to.

Do as much preliminary research as you can about the subjects you intend to bring up during the interview—after all, you don't want to sound like an idiot. Do your expert the courtesy of knowing *something* so he's not expected to divulge every aspect of his job, start to finish, during this one interview. It's best if you only ask him to fill in the few holes left after you've done your own research. If you've got a fairly good idea how long the outlining process will take, make an appointment with the expert you've chosen to interview for around the time of the outline's completion. This helps ensure that your list of questions is thorough and current.

Go over the list of interview questions often as you work on your outline, eliminating those you answer for yourself through research and adding those that crop up during outlining. Revise the questions for clarity if necessary. Include the chapter and/or scene numbers next to each question on your list. That way, when you're done with the interview, you can just drop the answers into the outline. Here's an example of an interview questions worksheet I created as I was outlining *Tears on Stone*, the second book in the Falcon's Bend mystery series, with my writing partner, Chris Spindler.

## INTERVIEW QUESTIONS
## TITLE: *TEARS ON STONE*

**QUESTION 1:** How do you run a sketch that your sketch artist has done of a suspect and find a match? Do you put it in the computer with a scanner and run it through some kind of program set up for this purpose? Does a regular PD have the kind of equipment necessary to match up the sketch, or do they send out for it? Do they mail or fax it to DCI? If they know exactly where to look for the match, how long would it take to get the match? How long would it take if you had no idea? Who does the match? The officer looking for the information? The investigator? Patrol officer? Dispatch? What if it's a case where the suspect isn't from the area, you know who the person is, and you actually know where he's from, but you have to prove it?

**Chapter(s)/page(s) where answer is needed:** chapter 55, page 127 and chapter 56, page 130 of the outline

**Facts or information I may need during the interview:** The suspect isn't from the area, but the detectives know where she hails from.

**Answer:**

**QUESTION 2:** How many years in prison would a person serve for armed robbery, and when might he be paroled?

**Chapter(s)/page(s) where answer is needed:** chapters 20 and 23 of the outline

**Facts or information I may need during the interview:** He planned and executed a robbery of a large bank. The robbery went wrong. One of the *thieves* was killed, but no one else was harmed. They were essentially caught in the act. He's been in jail for about 15 years. He's convicted on two to three? counts of armed robbery. He has no other misdemeanors or felonies on his record. Would it be realistic to say he's served 15 years, at which point (when the book opens) he gets parole? He's been a model prisoner. Generally, it's 3 months off every year of sentencing for model prisoners, isn't it? My research indicates that the penalty range for a robbery is 3 to 5 years. Most states have a law that requires a mandatory minimum term in prison if a firearm was used during the robbery. This term is in addition to the crime itself since armed robbery and most burglaries are felonies.

**Answer:**

Whenever you interview an expert, it's helpful to use a personal tape recorder (I know I can't write quickly or neatly enough, and I certainly can't rely on my memory). Once the interview is complete, transcribe your notes and file them in your research folder. Since the notes may be useful for other books as well, it's a good idea to make a hard copy you can insert into a large binder with similar research on the subject.

I won't tell you *how much* to research because there are already countless books out there on this subject, and, ultimately, that's up to you to decide. You'll know you've done your research well when you can write about everything in your book intelligently, without questioning anything.

## ADDITIONAL OUTLINE AIDS

Now that you've completed your preliminary outline and research, it's time to dig a little a deeper. Before you begin work on your formatted outline in Stage 4 of the 30-day method, review Worksheets 9–14 in Appendix C. These worksheets address key issues, such as dialogue, character and plot facts, and timelines. They will provide a crucial foundation for a more detailed outline, and they will help you stay organized as your outline becomes more complex.

Try to keep all the worksheets with your outline in your working project folder. (You may prefer to use a binder so you can separate the material by subject and refer to it easily as you work.) If you find that you're just not ready to fill out all the information on these worksheets, do read over the blank worksheets and allow the questions to percolate.

Please note that the outline aid worksheets provided for your use in Appendix C are formatted to inspire you to begin filling them out, but most of the time you'll simply do them free-form, as I have in the examples provided.

## Dialogue Worksheets

It's never too soon to start thinking about what your characters will say and how they'll say it. Providing each of your characters with a distinct and personalized voice is key to writing great fiction. The goal of the Worksheet 9 is to encourage you to think about your characters' individual speech patterns and specific word choices. Your characters will probably reveal such distinctions to you as your story progresses, but by thinking about it early, you'll be more open to such revelations.

For each of your major characters, record information about individual speech patterns and repeating catch phrases they may use. With this information in place on a dialogue sheet, you'll know exactly what a given character will say and how he'll say it. I also use this worksheet during the final edit and polish of the manuscript, just to double-check that everything is the way it should be.

Here's an example of a dialogue sheet I created for my novel *Degrees of Separation*. Please note that all of the examples in this chapter are from my own work. In some cases, I have altered the names and places so as not to give away anything important, in case you want to read the books. Because I recorded this information free-form, the sample dialogue sheet below will not look exactly like Worksheet 9 in Appendix C.

DIALOGUE SHEET
TITLE: *DEGREES OF SEPARATION*

**Character:** Ezra
**Dialogue specifics:** slang with gonna, wanna, there're; various
**Common expressions:** hell; God almighty

**Character:** Clarice
**Dialogue specifics:** slang sparingly, but New Orleans phrases:

lagniappe (lan'yap) = something extra for free

soc au' lai (sock-o-lay) = what the? wow! ouch!

where y'at? or y'ats? = how are you today?

beaucoup crasseux (boo-coo-cra-sue) = very dirty

| | |
|---|---|
| **Character:** | Eve |
| **Dialogue specifics:** | very proper, very southern belle; when Eve says "I," you should hear "ah," my = ma, I'm = ahm, time = tahm, really = rhully, why = wahh |
| **Common expressions:** | good gracious; I swear (to you); gosh |

## Fact Sheets

As your outline develops, it can become harder to keep track of everything—especially once you've added in all the factual information based on your research. A fact sheet (Worksheet 10 in Appendix C) can help you chart all crucial bits of information to ensure that the heart of your story remains consistent from outline to outline and draft to draft.

For example, if you're writing a mystery (especially if it's part of a series), you may want to keep track of when the main investigator first became a detective at this police department, how long he's been a detective, how many employees are in the department, etc. While you may have listed this type of information on the character sheet you filled out as part of your preliminary outline in chapter two, this new worksheet merges that information with other crucial details. Consolidating this information now will prove helpful as you begin your formatted outline and expand on your story.

Here's an example from a fact sheet I completed for *Degrees of Separation.*

FACT SHEET
TITLE: *DEGREES OF SEPARATION*

**LOCAL TOWN AND CHARACTER FACTS**

| Page or Chapter | Character | Location | Fact |
|---|---|---|---|
| page 7 | Police Department staff | Police Department | Police department employs: 12 full-time patrol officers (including Jensen, Bradley, Rosch, Folksmeyer); 6 reserves; patrol sergeant (Chopp); chief (Vanderwyst); administrative assistant (Maggie Sheppard); 2 investigators (Ezra & Ben). |

| Page or Chapter | Character | Location | Fact |
|---|---|---|---|
| page 42 | | | The high school in Falcon's Bend is called Falcon High. |
| page 82 | | | There are five blocks between the nightclub and Blaine's house. |
| page 87 | | Witmer Park | The park borders businesses on all sides; woods in the back, past the field—woods go back for at least a mile or more. |
| page 105 | | | The *Falcon's Bend Chronicle* is a weekly paper (it comes out on Monday). |

## SCENE OF THE CRIME/SUSPECT FACTS

| Page or Chapter | Character | Location | Fact |
|---|---|---|---|
| page 30 | | | Nightclub hours of operation: 7 P.M.–7 A.M., Mon.–Sat.; 7 P.M.–2 A.M., Sun. |
| page 36, 43 | Clarice and Cindy; Terry and Rox; Crystal and Lori | nightclub dressing rooms | Clarice and Cindy share dressing room 1; Terry and Rox share dressing room 2; Crystal and Lori share dressing room 3. |
| page 38 | Blaine | Blaine's home | Blaine's address is 519 Butler Circle. |
| page 173 | Crystal | | Crystal is from Metaire, LA. |
| page 173 | Blaine | | Blaine is from New Orleans, LA. |
| page 173 | Don | | Don is from Harlem, NY. |
| page 173 | Lori | | Lori is from East New Orleans (black projects). |
| page 173 | Cindy | | Cindy is from reservation near Charenton in St. Mary Parish. |
| page 173 | Rox | | Rox is from Brooklyn, NY. |
| page 173 | Terry (female) | | Terry is from East New Orleans (black projects). |
| page 173 | Clarice | | Clarice is from Esplanade Avenue in New Orleans. |
| page 173 | Eve | | Eve is from New Orleans (rich neighborhood, unspecified at any point but assumed). |

# Timeline Sheets

Timeline sheets keep track of the major events or character backgrounds within your story. Many of the facts will be for your eyes only, but recording them won't be a wasted effort. Your timeline sheets will aid in keeping everything straight and consistent.

## Background Timelines

Background timelines can be written for any character in your story. It's usually best to start with a defining moment in the character's life, an event that proved to be a pivotal in some way. While the information in a timeline may never appear in your finished novel, it can still influence how you tell your story. On the other hand, timeline information may turn out to play a crucial role in your story. For example, in Dennis Lehane's *Mystic River*, it's easy to spot background timeline events—and their effects on the characters throughout the novel.

This type of timeline is generally written free-form, but Worksheet 11 in Appendix C should get you started. If you find that the formatted worksheet hinders your creative process or inadvertently takes your story in directions you don't want it to go, then write the information down free-form as I've done in the example below.

For the outline of the third book of the Falcon's Bend series, *The Fifteenth Letter*, it was very important that I know the whole backstory of three major players in the book. I went right back to their childhoods in order to give myself an overall history of what they'd been through and specifics on the major events in their lives. Here's a portion of what I ended up with.

BACKGROUND TIMELINE
TITLE: *THE FIFTEENTH LETTER*

### AMBER'S CHILDHOOD

Zeke (19) gets Violet (16) pregnant. At the time, he's working part time at a handmade furniture factory. Zeke and Violet marry. Nine months later, Amber is born. Zeke is a wonderful father to his "Elfy," and he absolutely adores his little girl. He teaches her a love of puzzles (brainteaser puzzles like the Rubik's Cube and the interlocking wood types, where you have to figure out how to open it, etc.). He reads her The Lord of the Rings trilogy when she's only four. She falls completely in love with this book and the maps included. She and her father pour over these maps, then move on to others. Together, the two of them memorize and use Tolkien's Elvish language so no one else can listen to their conversations. Though she's close to her mother, Amber is a daddy's girl—her father is almost her entire life. She believes he's the ultimate good in the world, and her love for him is complete.

Zeke has the brain of an inventor. He and Amber designed—on paper—this globe puzzle (described in outline). Though the map on the globe is modern, it'll be "aged" to look like an ancient map. The point is to figure out how to open the globe. He later comes up with the idea of turning it into a safe.

All this time, Zeke has been working full time at the handmade furniture factory, but he's growing increasingly restless. He hates the 9-to-5 routine—his paycheck is barely enough to cover their living expenses, as Violet doesn't work. She stays home to care for Amber full time. Coming home to his family is all that keeps him sane. Whenever he's at work, all he thinks about is escape. He thinks frequently of easy money. He and Violet are very much in love, and she senses his unhappiness, but he refuses to admit it. While Zeke can't stand the thought of continuing at this job, he makes almost nothing for money, he hates the thought of allowing Violet to see his unhappiness even more. . . .

The complete timeline for Amber goes on for several pages, but only small portions of this information actually appear in the finished novel. The purpose of this background was simply to get it all straight in my own (and my partner's) mind to help us understand where the characters came from and why they became the people they were at the time the story began. I was able to write the first pass of the book with a sense of richness I wouldn't have had without sketching it all out this way.

Writing a background timeline is a lot like writing a preliminary outline. In some cases, you may be able to use a lot of what you come up with in your story. In other cases, the events happened well before the actual story began and the reader only needs to know certain parts of it.

## Miscellaneous Timelines

A miscellaneous timeline (Worksheet 12 in Appendix C) is used to keep track of miscellaneous events that occur before or during the actual story and that are important to the story. Record the page numbers for each fact so you can use the worksheet as a handy reference while you outline, write, or perform editor revisions. Here's an example of the miscellaneous timeline sheet I used for *Degrees of Separation*.

### MISCELLANEOUS TIMELINE
### TITLE: *DEGREES OF SEPARATION*

**GENERAL CHARACTER TIMELINE**

| Page or Chapter | Character | Location | Timeline Fact |
|---|---|---|---|
| page 5 | Annie and Ezra | | They've been married for 2 years. |
| page 7 | | Falcon's Bend town | The last murder in the town took place 2 years ago. |
| page 8 | | nightclub | The nightclub opened 8 months ago. |

| Page or Chapter | Character | Location | Timeline Fact |
|---|---|---|---|
| page 42 | Ben | | He returned to town "a few years ago." |
| page 85 | Terry | nightclub and Witmer Park | It takes 12 minutes to get from the nightclub to Witmer Park, so if Terry left the nightclub at 3:15, she'd reach the park by 3:30 at the latest. |
| page 89 | Eve, Clarice, Blaine | | Eve and Clarice met Blaine 3 years ago when they were 19. |
| pages 119, 208 | Blaine | Blaine's home and Witmer Park | It takes 13 minutes to get from Blaine's to Witmer Park by car and 30 minutes by foot. |
| pages 164, 258 | Blaine | Los Angeles | Blaine and troupe surface in L.A. |
| page 335 | Clarice (Eve/ Blaine) | Los Angeles | Clarice went to live with Eve and Eve's father when she was 18 (4 years ago), just before Blaine and troupe moved to Los Angeles. |

## Crime Timelines for Mystery and Suspense Novels

If you're writing a mystery or suspense novel, you need to keep track of the who, what, where, and when of the crimes central to your story. With a crime timeline (Worksheet 13 in Appendix C), you can record exactly how crimes were committed and by whom, the exact time, the place, and the possible witnesses to the deed. You should include both the actual facts of the event and witness accounts. You won't necessarily show your reader all of this in a linear fashion, but this worksheet will help you keep all your facts in order as you decide what information will be dropped into your outline and where. Here's another example from *Degrees of Separation*.

### CRIME TIMELINE
### TITLE: *DEGREES OF SEPARATION*

**Victim:** Terry

**Details of Death:** Terry has been dead less than 12 hours; time of death: between 2 A.M. and 4:30 A.M. If Terry died at 3:30, she'd been killed only a few minutes after reaching Witmer Park since she left the club at 3:15 and it took around 12 minutes to reach Witmer's parking lot.

## FIRST MURDER (ACTUAL WITNESS ACCOUNT)

| Page or Chapter | Character/ Suspect | Location at the Time of the Crime | Day and Time | Specific Information |
|---|---|---|---|---|
| page 33 | Lori | nightclub | Wednesday, 2:30 A.M. | Lori was on her break, looking for her syrup of ipecac. |
| page 31 | Don | nightclub | Wednesday, after 3 A.M. | Don was kicking out an unruly customer. |
| page 47 | Rox | nightclub | Wednesday, 3:15 A.M. | Rox says Terry left the nightclub. |
| page 57 | Lori/Lance | nightclub | Wednesday, 3:30–6 A.M. | Lori was in her dressing room with Lance. |
| page 33 | Blaine | nightclub | Thursday, 5 A.M. | He claims he was closing up the nightclub and was in his office all last night. |

## NIGHTCLUB EMPLOYEE BREAKS AFTER 2 A.M.

| Page or Chapter | Character/ Suspect | Location at the Time of the Crime | Day and Time | Specific Information |
|---|---|---|---|---|
| | Cindy | nightclub/room 1 | 2 A.M. | |
| | Clarice | nightclub/room 1 | 2:15 A.M. | |
| | Lori | nightclub/room 3 | 2:30 A.M. | |
| | Crystal | nightclub/room 3 | 2:45 A.M. | |
| | Terry | nightclub/room 2 | 3 A.M. | |
| | Rox | nightclub/room 2 | 3:15 A.M. | |
| | Cindy | nightclub/room 1 | 3:30 A.M. | |
| | Clarice | nightclub/room 1 | 3:45 A.M. | |
| | | | 4 A.M. | Nightclub closes. |

## KILLER'S TIMELINE (FOR AUTHOR'S EYES ONLY)

| Page or Chapter | Character/ Suspect | Location at the Time of the Crime | Day and Time | Specific Information |
|---|---|---|---|---|
| | killer | nightclub/ dressing rooms 2 and 3 | 2:15 A.M. | During first dance break, the killer sneaks into dressing room 3 and gets Lori's ipecac, then sneaks into dressing room 2 and poisons Terry's snack. |
| | killer | nightclub bar | 3 A.M. | At the bar, the killer stages an argument with a customer. |

| Page or Chapter | Character/ Suspect | Location at the Time of the Crime | Day and Time | Specific Information |
|---|---|---|---|---|
| | Terry/Rox | nightclub | 3 A.M. | Terry has her break. Rox is just getting ready for her next dance. Terry takes a bite, is sick. Rox goes looking for Don so he can take Terry home, but he's busy dealing with the noisy patron (that's why the killer picked on him in the first place). |
| | killer | nightclub bar | just after 3 A.M. | The killer complains to Don, who comes to kick the guy out. |
| | Terry/Rox | nightclub | just after 3 A.M. | Rox tells Terry Don can't drive her home right now. Terry, who's feeling much better already, says the fresh air will do her good and decides to walk home. |
| | killer/Terry | the walk home between the nightclub and Witmer Park | 3:15 A.M. | The killer takes off shoes and leaves through the back door. Terry is walking in front, slowly, unsteady. |
| | killer/Terry | Witmer Park | 3:30 A.M. | They reach the playground. The killer strangles Terry and runs back, arrives just in time for second break. |

## Motives and Alibis for Mystery and Suspense Novels

Keep track of your characters' motives and alibis using Worksheet 14 in Appendix C. My writing partner, Chris Spindler, created this nifty little worksheet while we were outlining and writing one of the books in our Falcon's Bend series. There were two murders, so we created a separate worksheet for each victim. The example below is the worksheet we completed for Crystal's murder, the second in the book.

MOTIVES AND ALIBIES WORKSHEET
TITLE: *DEGREES OF SEPARATION*

| Suspect | Motive | Alibi |
|---------|--------|-------|
| Blaine | She thought he would run away with her, so she put him under pressure. | Around midnight at the club, when Lori sprained her ankle, he was there; still, she could have sneaked out, drove home, killed Crystal, all in less than twenty minutes. |
| Don | ? | At the club, dealing with a scheduling nightmare; was seen by his staff and the dancers. |
| Rox | Jealousy, hate for Blaine and her "competition"; thinks it would hurt Blaine to kill one of them. | None; she could have been there when it happened and then run away; strong suspect. |
| Clarice | In competition with the other girls for Blaine's affections. | Says she had a date; alibi cannot be verified at this time. |
| Eve | Is she trying to destroy Blaine by killing all his dancers? | None, but she was at the nightclub when it happened; says she can't remember. |

Using these outline aids can be extremely helpful for you at any point in your outlining, writing, or editing process. These worksheets can even come in handy after you sell the book, because they'll help you stay organized and consistent while doing revisions for your publisher.

*With your research for the outline complete and the outline aid worksheets started, let's move on to Stage 3 of the 30-day method: Story Evolution.*

# CHAPTER FOUR

# Days 14–15:
# The Evolution of Your Story

Each story has a beginning, a middle, and an end. Sounds simple, but the road from beginning to middle to end isn't always as easy to navigate as it sounds. Many experienced writers believe that the first fifty or so pages of a novel are the easiest to write. Setting up a story and its characters takes very little forethought or talent. Even those who have never written a book before will find the beginning of a book fairly simple to draft. The end of a book is another fairly easy task. Ask any author about the earliest concept she had of a given novel, and most likely she will say she knew how it would end before she wrote a word of it—coming up with a grand and glorious finale was anything but a hardship.

The problems usually start popping up around the middle of the book. Hands down, this is the hardest section to write. Unfortunately, it's also usually the longest section of the book.

Why is the middle so difficult? Because it's where your novel's true mettle is tested. If your story structure is lacking, the middle of the book will reveal these cracks to you in black and white. You know where your story threads start and where they should end up, but it's tricky to track those threads through what can be a murky, dark course.

In this chapter, we're going to discuss how every memorable, well-constructed story evolves through each of the three sections of a book (beginning, middle, and end). This steady, logical evolution is the basic framework of any strong novel and will form the structure of the formatted outline you'll begin in the next chapter. This framework is what will make up the invisible, unshakable foundation of your story. If you learn to see this structure in other novels, it will be easier to construct in your own.

### Stage 3: Story Evolution

| Schedule | What to Complete |
|----------|------------------|
| **Days 14–15** | Fill Out the Story Evolution Worksheet |

Total: 2 days to the framework of a solid story

The preliminary outline you completed in chapter two stated your novel's basic premise, conflicts, and issues that need to be resolved. The plot sketch further detailed these points. Now it's time to complete your story evolution worksheet (Worksheet 15 in Appendix C). This worksheet is broken down into three parts (beginning, middle, and end), so you can take a logical and much more detailed approach to weaving your plot threads through your book from start to finish. Keep your plot sketch from chapter two in mind as you fill out the story evolution worksheet. By the time you complete this worksheet, your plot threads should be firmly enmeshed with the story evolution framework.

Story evolution is a process of brainstorming, and therefore it tends to be anything but linear. Work through the story evolution worksheet in whatever way you feel led by your muse. Again, you'll be provided with tips throughout the story evolution process to help you work more clearly and efficiently.

We'll be using examples from three popular books to fill out samples of the beginning section, the middle section, and the end section of a story evolution worksheet. If you're interested in seeing each section of the story evolution worksheet filled out for a single novel, visit my Web site (www.karenwiesner.com) and click on "First Draft."

## THE BEGINNING

Plots, subplots, characters, goals, and conflicts are introduced in the beginning of a story. Your goal is to pull the reader in with an exciting opening, then begin setting up the basis for the rest of the book. Depending on the length and complexity of your story, the beginning generally amounts to about the first fifty pages.

The beginning of your story is where you introduce your main characters' attributes and motivations. The qualities you give your characters are what makes the reader care about them. Your characters' behavior, reactions, and introspection, as well as their ever-evolving goals, draw sympathy and interest from the reader. The main characters in your story don't have to be the moral equivalent of Snow White, either. Even character flaws and sins can draw the reader's sympathy. Why? Because flaws make the hero more real in the reader's mind. The reader understands and forgives because she can relate to these very human flaws.

From a reader's standpoint, the only difference between a hero and a villain is the reader's ability to forgive one and not the other. Both heroes and villains are human (unless you're writing a horror or paranormal story), both have a unique combination of good and bad traits, and both should be fleshed out enough to become real to the reader. The hero, however, will behave and develop in such a way that the reader will forgive all flaws. The villain will not earn forgiveness.

**For every action a character takes, there is a response from the reader:**

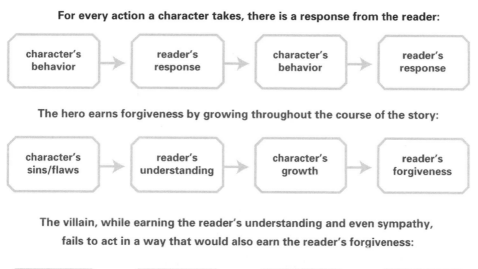

**The hero earns forgiveness by growing throughout the course of the story:**

**The villain, while earning the reader's understanding and even sympathy, fails to act in a way that would also earn the reader's forgiveness:**

For a story to sustain the reader's sympathy, the hero must be understood and forgiven by the reader. This will only happen if the hero has a noble reason for any crimes. (A villain should also have a reason for his crimes, but his reason doesn't have to be noble.) The hero must also show marked growth throughout the course of the story, thereby redeeming himself for any human weaknesses. (The villain never repents or redeems himself.) There are, of course, always exceptions to these rules.

Don't be afraid to get inside your characters—revealing their most heinous thoughts and secrets along with their most noble ones—in order to create compassion in your readers. It's important to think about your characters' conflicts, motivations, intentions, and weaknesses right from the start. As the outlining process grows more intense, your insights into your characters will deepen, and your finished manuscript will be the better for it.

## Conflict

Your reader needs to be assured from your very first sentence that something suspenseful and exciting is happening or about to happen. Conflict is the root of everything exciting and suspenseful in your story.

What are conflict and suspense, how do they work, and how do you create them? Conflict can be internal or external. Each of your main characters should have internal conflicts—opposing desires, beliefs, or motivations. External conflict can (and should) occur between characters, but characters can conflict with other things as well (like fate or

Mother Nature). A solid plot gives *all* main characters (including the villain) internal and external conflicts.

For example, imagine your hero desperately loves your heroine. The heroine, however, is engaged to someone else. Your hero has an internal conflict: He wants to express his love, but he must respect the heroine's choice . . . at least for now.

There is also an external conflict between the hero and the heroine's fiancé—they each want the love of the heroine. Both the internal and external conflicts will create tension and suspense. Will the hero overcome his internal objections and declare his love? Will the heroine realize she's with the wrong person?

Now imagine the heroine is engaged to the villain. When the treachery of the villain is revealed to the hero, the hero *must* take action. But if the heroine doesn't discover the villain's evil ways at the same time, she and the hero may come into conflict when the hero tries to save her. When characters or circumstances conflict, the result is action—and action is exciting to the reader. Uncertainty over the outcome of the action is suspense.

There's another way to look at it. In order to develop both plot and character, you need to give your characters both internal and external reasons to act in the face of conflict. In the example above, the hero's love for the heroine is his internal reason to act, and the villain's treachery is the external reason. There are internal and external obstacles in the path of the hero as well: The hero's wish to respect the choice of the heroine (or at least not to anger her) is the internal obstacle, and the danger presented by the villain is the external one. By using both internal and external motivations and obstacles in your story, you create suspense, excitement, and a hero who won't simply give up in the face of a monumental challenge.

The time to incorporate conflict and suspense into your novel is now. Your formatted outline should contain both of these elements as they will appear in your book, which is why Stage 3 of the 30-day method is dedicated to story evolution. Be sure to lay the groundwork for conflict in the beginning section of your outline.

Keep the following tips in mind when building opportunities for action and suspense into the beginning of your story:

1. Keep the reader on edge with baffling contrasts in characters, setting, and dialogue. If you put two seemingly opposed characters in play together, you'll intrigue your readers and they will stick around to figure out why.
2. Take advantage of pacing, especially as you move toward and through the middle of your story. Don't rush in to pick up the story threads. Keep the reader guessing. Draw out scenes involving rescues and explanations. Offer the reader unsatisfactory alternatives to problems. Alternate suspense and action within your outline, even if just by giving yourself stage directions for accomplishing this.

3. Carefully construct mood by using description, dialogue, introspection, and action. If you want to create a sensual atmosphere, describe the scent of a candle burning, the touch of silk against bare skin, the strains of romantic music playing, or a heroine's reaction to the appearance of her lover. If you want to set the mood for danger, make the character tangibly aware of the temperature (if it's cold, give the character goose bumps), the lighting (darkness or shadows), a revolting smell, a sudden sound, or the eerie *absence* of sound.

4. Use foreshadowing: a whispered conversation, an event that has no satisfying explanation, an unexpected expression or reaction from a character that reveals he may not be who he claims to be. Foreshadowing shouldn't answer the crucial questions of a story, but instead create possibilities or uncertainties that will evoke mild or extreme tension in the reader.

Conflict, suspense, and motivation will be the driving forces behind your story. Lay the groundwork for them in your outline, and they will reach their full potential in your story. Remember: Never allow the reader to get too cozy.

Now that we've reviewed the fundamentals of writing a good beginning, let's discuss the first section of the story evolution worksheet.

### 1. Conflict Is Introduced

Most writers have been advised to begin each story with a bang. There's good reason for that. You want to hook your reader as early as possible. Detail here what will happen in your prologue or first scene, and briefly describe how the conflict you introduce at this point will dominate your story through each section. Also, be sure to hint at looming conflicts. As your beginning progresses, you'll want to fully introduce the villain or threat.

### 2. Story Goal Is Introduced

The story goal, as discussed in chapter two, is your dominant plot thread. You will introduce it in the beginning of the book. Review your plot sketch worksheet from your preliminary outline (Worksheet 4 in Appendix C), then describe the story goal and how it will push your story forward through each section.

### 3. Characters Are Outfitted for Their Tasks

The character sketches you created in chapter two as part of your preliminary outline will help you continue to think about who your main characters are and how they're involved in achieving the story's goal.

Your characters should be designed with the resolution of the story goal in mind. They should have strengths they themselves aren't aware of at the beginning of the story—strengths that evolve steadily throughout the course of the book as the characters face adversity. They also should have internal and/or external weaknesses that hinder their progress. Detail these things in this section.

As you think about the first fifty or so pages that set up the premise of your book, continue to expand on the three points we just covered. These points will help you come up with everything you need to keep your audience reading voraciously.

Now, let's look at an example of a completed story evolution worksheet for the beginning portion of *Out of the Dark* by Sharon Sala. In the example, notice how conflict, goal, and characters are firmly established and already evolving:

## STORY EVOLUTION
## TITLE: *OUT OF THE DARK*

### PART I: THE BEGINNING

#### 1. Conflict Is Introduced

**Detail the major conflict:** Margaret Cochrane has been lured into the clutches of a religious cult called the People of Joy and into the hands of its evil but seductive leader, Solomon (alias for the story villain Otis Jacks). In the middle of the night, Margaret takes her four-year-old daughter Jade and leaves her husband to run away with the People of Joy.

Otis's crimes come back to haunt him 20 years later when Jade becomes a media darling after the ordeal she went through under the twisted leadership of Solomon, and one of Otis's former customers (a famed politician) is in danger of being exposed for his pedophile tendencies.

#### 2. Story Goal Is Introduced

**Detail the major story goal:** Twenty years after Jade's abduction, she and Rafael—who were used and sexually exploited by the People of Joy throughout their childhoods—have escaped, but are living their lives on the run, terrified of being found by Solomon. Sam Cochrane, Jade's father, has spent 20 years and countless dollars searching for his missing wife and daughter.

Jade is an artist. A painting of her dead mother is recognized at a street fair and purchased by the wife of Jade's father's closest friend. Though Jade and her companion flee once again, Sam is finally reunited with his daughter by ex-police officer Luke Kelly. Jade has been scarred profoundly by the ordeal she's lived through. Just as Jade is beginning a new life, a life that could allow her to heal, the reconciliation between father and daughter comes to national attention. Solomon/Otis Jacks must cover up the crimes Jade could expose, and her healing and very existence is threatened.

**3. Characters Are Outfitted for Their Tasks**

**List and briefly describe the characters who will be involved in reaching the story goal and defeating the conflict. Detail each character's strengths and weaknesses:**

1. Raphael, Jade's companion. Jade is Raphael's only family, the only good part of his life—a life that is coming to an end as the horrors of his childhood claim him. All Raphael wants is to see that Jade is protected when he's gone.

2. Sam Cochrane, Jade's father. He will protect with his very life the daughter he'd loved with all his heart before she was stolen from him.

3. Luke Kelly. For the first time in her life, Jade is learning what love—true, pure, healing love between a man and a woman—can be like with Luke.

# THE MIDDLE

If you haven't already, review the plot sketch worksheet (Worksheet 4 in Appendix C) you began while creating your preliminary outline. It's time to develop your plot sketch to the next level as you outline the evolution of the middle portion of your book.

The middle is usually the largest portion of any book. In this section, plots, subplots, and conflicts work together to create a tug-of-war between the story goal and the opposition. Essentially, the action in the middle section of a book revolves around the main characters confronting the opposition, though most of the time this opposition is hidden from or unseen by the lead characters.

Your main characters must grow throughout this section of the book, proving themselves worthy opponents to the villains. Therefore, each of the events that take place within this section will require multiple scenes to work *in* and work *out*. In other words, you will be planning multiple scenes for each pull in the tug-of-war between your main characters and their opposition. The longer your book, the more complex this tug-of-war will be.

You could look at the middle section of a book as a series of actions and reactions. Your characters will react to conflict by creating short-term goals to get them through it. Characters will set new short-term goals throughout the book based on the experiences and emotions they go through. In almost all cases, old short-term goals will be revised or new ones created in response to a failure (or thwarting) of the original goals. Because all of these short-term goals work toward the resolution of the story goal, there will be a unifying theme to the middle section of the book, preventing it from appearing disjointed.

To maintain logic and flow throughout the middle of a book, it's important to show both action and reaction for every conflict. Each action produces a reaction, and each reaction justifies the next action. Every step your characters take depends on the previous step.

The character's reactions must match the intensity of the conflict. Keep in mind that reaction adds to the depth and dimension of the story characters. Since most people initially freak out in reaction to conflict (a commonality that helps build a bridge of empathy between character and reader), your characters may have an initial crazed reaction before they calm down and reason takes over, enabling them to focus on the next short-term goal. Your readers will root for a character with the ability to conquer fear with reason.

The crazed reaction stage is the ideal time to take a short break in the action and tension to reveal to the reader what could happen if the characters fail to reach the next step toward the story goal. In other words, the crazed reaction provides the perfect opportunity for downtime, which should occur near the end of the middle section of the book. It's during downtime that a main character reflects on his desires and motivations, imagining a happily-ever-after that is out of reach because of the obstacles presented in the book. At this point, the character may decide that attaining his goals is impossible, and it would be best to give up the fight. Or, he may have a "damn it all; I'm taking what I want, not thinking about what I have to do" attitude during this time. Finally, the character decides on a course of action, creating new short-term goals in an effort to bring about the desired resolution. This will be his final, desperate attempt to reach the story goal. In some cases, the character will decide to act because the stakes of the conflict are again raised—danger is near, and he must move forward whether he wants to or not. The new danger propels the story to the next level.

It's essential that a character's actions propel him forward, even when short-term goals and conflicts make it seem like he's not making any headway toward the story goal. That's part of the tug-of-war that keeps the reader immersed in the story. Continue to raise the stakes between the main characters and the opposition. The opposition must become more and more of a threat to the story goal, creating more of a challenge as the main character attempts to reach the story goal in multiple ways by devising short-term goals to get him there.

In these concluding scenes of the middle of the book, downtime must be followed with a black moment. Downtime releases the tension for a short period, and that tension must be built back up quickly or you risk losing your reader.

Here's how the story evolution worksheet helps you plan out the middle of your book:

### 1. Characters Design Short-Term Goals to Reach the Story Goal

For each main character, introduce short-term goals that will assist that character in reaching the story goal. Give a brief description of each goal and how each character is attempting to reach it. Use your plot sketch (Worksheet 4 in Appendix C) as a springboard for this section.

### 2. Quest to Reach the Story Goal Begins

In this section, the characters put their first short-term goals into action. Sketch out what they go through during this time.

### 3. First Short-Term Goals Are Thwarted

The first short-term goal proves impossible. What events take place to make this failure come about?

### 4. Characters React With Disappointment

Characters react differently to disappointment, and these reactions show the kind of people they are. Provide insight into each major character's reactions.

### 5. Stakes of the Conflict Are Raised

Giving up the quest to reach the story goal is never really an option, though the characters may wish they could. In every exciting story with worthy heroes, something always happens to make it impossible to concede defeat. Inevitably, the stakes are raised and a new danger is introduced; the threat is immediate, and the hero can't simply ignore or walk away from it. Detail the new danger and its effect on all subplots.

### 6. Characters React to the Conflict

In this section, describe each main character's initial reaction to the new danger or problem. This is often the "freak out" stage, where few are capable of being rational.

### 7. Characters Revise Old or Design New Short-Term Goals

Though the initial reaction to the danger is usually one that's far from calm and logical, this must be a temporary reaction. Eventually, each main character will need to devise a new short-term goal to lead him closer to reaching the story goal. Briefly describe each character's plan of action.

### 8. Quest to Reach the Story Goal Is Continued

The characters put their new short-term goals in action. In this section, sketch out what they go through during this time.

### 9. Short-Term Goals Are Again Thwarted

The new short-term goals prove as impossible as the first. What events took place to make this failure come about?

### 10. Characters React With Disappointment

Character reactions will run the gamut here, but each character will be tiring of the battle a little more each time he fails. Restlessness to get closer to the story goal works to create edgier personalities.

### 11. Stakes of the Conflict Are Raised

Remember that each time something happens, it must create ever more dire consequences if the characters don't act quickly.

### 12. Characters React to the Conflict

Show marked growth in the characters, even if it seems as though they're making no progress in reaching the ultimate story goal. Make the readers emphasize with them, root for them, and possibly even love them.

*At this stage in the middle of your story, you can repeat the following steps (items seven through ten as discussed previously) as many times as necessary to accommodate your story's length and complexity:*

- *characters revise old or create new short-term goals*
- *the quest to reach the story goal continues*
- *short-term goals are thwarted*
- *characters react with disappointment*

*Items eleven and twelve aren't repeated here because the cycle becomes more dramatic with each repetition, thus allowing the last half of the middle portion of your book to be even tenser and your characters more desperate. Even if your characters revise their goals and continue onward, they no longer have any confidence that they'll actually reach their goal, thus setting up the looming downtime.*

### 13. Downtime Begins

The last section of the middle portion of the story begins with the downtime, which precedes the black moment. Here, your characters are close to giving up for good because the story goal seems impossible to reach. At this critical point in the story, your characters are coming to feel they have nothing left to hold on to. Detail these feelings.

### 14. Characters Revise Old or Design New Short-Term Goals With Renewed Vigor

Your characters are going to make their next decisions out of sheer desperation. From this point on, they seem to lose much of their confidence—or worse, they're feeling a reckless sense of bravado that may have tragic consequences. What are their new goals and how do they plan to reach them?

### 15. The Quest to Reach the Story Goal Continues, But Instability Abounds

Though your characters are plowing ahead bravely, each step is taken with deep uncertainty. How does this action unfold?

### 16. The Black Moment Begins

The worst possible failure or horror that was introduced in the beginning of the book has now come to pass. The short-term goals made in desperation are thwarted, and the stakes are raised to fever pitch as the worst of all possible conflicts is unveiled. Describe it in as much detail as you can.

**17. The Characters React to the Black Moment**

Characters react to this major conflict with a sense of finality—the quest stands on the edge of a knife. Never will there be a moment when the outcome is more in question than in this concluding section of the middle of the book. Will evil triumph over good? That question won't be answered here; it belongs in the end section of the book.

Let's look at the middle section of the story evolution worksheet completed as it might have been for J.R.R. Tolkien's *The Lord of the Rings: The Fellowship of the Ring*. To avoid confusion, let's start at the point just past the initial introduction that sets up the story goal, the major conflict, and the characters. We'll stop at the end of the first book in the trilogy.

As you read through the example, notice how the conflicts evolve to nail-biting tension. If the middle section of your story is properly developed, nothing short of a natural catastrophe will be able to keep the reader from reading on to find out how the story will end.

## STORY EVOLUTION
### TITLE: *THE FELLOWSHIP OF THE RING*

**PART II. THE MIDDLE**

**1. Characters Design Short-Term Goals to Reach the Story Goal**

**Character 1:** Frodo Baggins

**Briefly describe his first short-term goal and how he'll go about reaching it:** The story goal is, of course, for the One Ring to be cast into the fires of Mount Doom. Frodo's first short-term goal is to take the Ring to Rivendell, to the house of Elrond, where it will be decided who will take the Ring to Mount Doom.

**Character 2:** Samwise Gamgee

**Briefly describe his first short-term goal and how he'll go about reaching it:** Sam is charged (by Gandalf the Wizard) with accompanying Frodo to Rivendell.

**Additional Characters:** Merry Brandybuck and Pippin Took

**Briefly describe their first short-term goal and how they'll go about reaching it:** These friends of Frodo and Sam will accompany them on their journey.

### 2. Quest to Reach the Story Goal Begins

**Briefly detail the events that take place:** Frodo, Sam, Merry, and Pippin begin the journey on foot, via the road.

### 3. First Short-Term Goals Are Thwarted

**Briefly detail the events that take place:** On the road, Black Riders are searching for the Ring. They pursue the companions. When they escape the Black Riders, there's a letter from Gandalf at The Prancing Pony, telling them that a ranger, Strider, will lead them to Rivendell, and that Gandalf will join them when he can. During the next leg of the journey, when Frodo puts the Ring on, the Black Riders are alerted to him and surround the travelers. Frodo is stabbed by the Black Rider King's knife.

### 4. Characters React With Disappointment

**Characters:** Frodo, Sam, Merry, and Pippin

**Briefly describe their reactions:** Fear over the Black Riders following them and Frodo's deadly wound, uncertainty that they'll ever reach Rivendell, and disappointment over Gandalf's failure to join them.

### 5. Stakes of the Conflict Are Raised

**Detail new stakes of the conflict and how they affect all subplots:** At Rivendell, Frodo is healed by Elrond and the companions are finally joined by Gandalf. Gandalf reveals to the Council that Saruman the White Wizard has joined the evil Sauron in his quest for domination.

### 6. Characters React to the Conflict

**Characters:** all

**Briefly describe the reaction to the conflict:** Dread. Evil will overtake them from all sides soon if the One Ring isn't destroyed—but getting it to Mount Doom could mean death. There is also much anger, and even some thoughts about using the One Ring to bring order. Common sense reigns as several present at the council meeting point out that the Ring brings only death.

### 7. Characters Revise Old or Design New Short-Term Goals

**Character 1:** Frodo

**Briefly describe his new short-term goal and how he'll go about reaching it:** Frodo bravely agrees to take the One Ring to Mount Doom and destroy it—though he doesn't know the way.

**Additional Characters:** A new company is formed to carry the One Ring to Mount Doom. The Fellowship of the Ring is made up of Gandalf, Frodo, Sam, Merry, Pippin, Strider, Gimli of Gloin, Boromir of Gondor, and Legolas the elf.

### 8. Quest to Reach the Story Goal Is Continued

**Briefly detail the events that take place:** They plan to take a path through the Dimrill Dale, climbing the Redhorn Gate Pass under Caradhras mountains into the vale of the Dwarves.

### 9. Short-Term Goals Are Again Thwarted

**Briefly detail the events that take place:** Winter on the mountaintop of Caradhras proves treacherous. The way is impassable.

### 10. Characters React With Disappointment

**Characters:** the Fellowship

**Briefly describe their reaction:** Shivering and miserable, they concede that they can't go forward. Therefore, they must go back.

### 11. Stakes of the Conflict Are Raised

**Detail new stakes of the conflict and how they affect all subplots:** The only choice, besides admitting defeat and returning to Rivendell without completing their quest, is to go through the Mines of Moria.

### 12. Characters React to the Conflict

**Characters:** the Fellowship

**Briefly describe the reactions to the conflict:** Dread, fear of this ancient place that's looked upon as evil.

*Note to readers: Items 7 through 10 repeat here. As I mentioned above, this section of the cycle can repeat several times throughout the course of your novel as your characters readjust their short-term goals in order to meet their objectives.*

### 7. Characters Revise Old or Design New Short-Term Goals

**Characters:** the Fellowship

**Briefly describe their new short-term goal and how they'll go about reaching it:** No one wants to go to this evil place, but there is no choice if they are to continue their quest.

### 8. Quest to Reach the Story Goal Is Continued

**Briefly detail the events that take place:** Once they reach the Walls of Moria, a password is required to open the Elven Door to the mines. Once they are over the Bridge of Khazad-dum, they are close to escape from the mines.

### 9. Short-Term Goals Are Again Thwarted

**Briefly detail the events that take place:** Orcs that live within the mines are alerted to the presence of the Fellowship by an unfortunate accident. An even greater threat presents itself—the Balrog, an ancient evil that only a Wizard can battle. Though Gandalf defeats the Balrog, he falls into the black pit after the creature.

### 10. Characters React With Disappointment

**Characters:** the remainder of the Fellowship

**Briefly describe reactions:** Devastation and grief for their lost companion settles on all of them once they escape the mines.

*Note to readers: The final cycle that begins with downtime starts here with item 13. Items 13 and 14 replace 11 and 12 in the previous cycle.*

### 13. Downtime Begins

**Detail the events that lead to downtime:** See item 9 in shaded box.

**Characters:** the remainder of the Fellowship

**Briefly describe their reaction to these events:** After seeing Gandalf fall to his death, the Fellowship believes there is no hope their quest will succeed. They proceed to Lothlorien, an elven village, where they rest as they grieve. Each is confronted with his greatest fears. Frodo looks into the mirror of the elf queen Galadriel and is shown the horrifying future should the Fellowship fail.

**14. Characters Revise Old or Design New Short-Term Goals With Renewed Vigor**

**Characters:** the remainder of the Fellowship

**Briefly describe desperate short-term goals and how they'll go about reaching them:** Celeborn, King of the Lothlorien Wood Elves, encourages the Fellowship to strengthen their wills and continue their quest. Gifts are given to each member of the Fellowship, and, with these tokens of hope, the company departs once more on the quest.

**15. The Quest to Reach the Story Goal Continues, But Instability Abounds**

**Briefly detail the events that take place:** The river Anduin is the group's means of travel as it continues toward Mordor, but the Fellowship is already beginning to break. The Ring is tearing the company apart with its evil desire to return to its master, Sauron, and the Fellowship is being tracked by its many enemies.

**16. The Black Moment Begins**

**Briefly detail the events that take place and how they affect all subplots:** Frodo knows now that he must continue the quest on his own at his first opportunity. Boromir attempts to take the Ring by force, and, to escape him, Frodo puts on the ring. The Eye of Sauron falls upon him. Knowing what he must do, Frodo rushes to the boats and attempts to depart from the company, but his faithful friend Sam insists on coming along.

**17. The Characters React to the Black Moment**

**Characters:** Frodo and Sam

**Briefly describe their reactions:** Grateful for each other's company in the rest of their quest, but terrified about what lies ahead. They believe they shall never see the rest of their companions, nor their beloved home in the Shire, again.

**Additional Characters:** what remains of the Fellowship

**Briefly describe their reaction:** The rest of the Fellowship is in great panic and madness. Merry and Pippin have disappeared in search of Frodo, and the rest have become scattered and lost. Evil may well overcome good.

## THE END

At the end of a book, all plots, subplots, and conflicts are resolved. Getting to that point—as we've just seen—should be a hair-raising ride that produces intense emotions in the reader. In the last few chapters of a book, the characters are finally given a well-deserved break from their recent crisis, and the reader can breathe a sigh of relief through smiles or tears. The end of the book will usually amount to a hundred pages, more or less.

Here's how the end of the book takes shape through the story evolution worksheet:

### 1. A Pivotal, Life-Changing Event Occurs

Something crucial must happen in the first part of the end section—something that will change the lives of the characters irrevocably and take them a millimeter from losing everything they hold dear. The main characters must become profoundly aware of everything they'll lose if the story goal isn't reached. This could be an injury or death. It could also be a terrifying experience of some kind that shakes the characters to their very cores.

### 2. Characters Modify Short-Term Goals One Last Time

Whatever the life-altering experience the characters face, the desperation that drove them only a few chapters earlier is completely gone. They've never had such clarity of purpose as they do at this moment. They know exactly what they have to do now, and absolutely nothing can stop them from doing it. One final time, they revise their goals with the kind of determination that convinces the reader they can't possibly fail.

### 3. The Showdown Begins

The main characters and opposition come face to face. There's no hiding as in the middle of the book. It's in these moments of confrontation that the main characters rise above the human state and become truly phenomenal as they move to accomplish the story goal.

### 4. The Opposition Is Vanquished and the Conflict Ends

You know the showdown that follows the moment of clarity very well. I'm sure most of you have an unforgettable story in mind where exactly this happened. Here's an example of such a heart-charging moment: In *Frankenstein*, the horrifying creature kills the doctor's beloved Elizabeth, and Dr. Frankenstein's fury drives him to pursue the creature to the ends of the earth. But he's unsuccessful in his purpose. When Dr. Frankenstein is on his deathbed, however, the creature comes to him in agony and self-reproach and ultimately kills himself.

### 5. The Story Goal Is Achieved

That which all the characters have been striving for has come to pass—hallelujah!—and this will affect everything. In this section, detail the consequences of victory to all plots and subplots.

### 6. Characters React to the Resolution of the Plot and Subplots

In this section, release is given to the characters who have worked so hard to achieve the story goal. Describe their reactions.

### 7. The *Relationship* Black Moment Is Addressed (Optional)

In a romance novel, the black moment in the relationship refers to the moment when the characters have to evaluate whether the resolution of the story goal has cleared the path toward togetherness for them. Despite the resolution of the story goal, this is the place to detail the bit of wavering that almost always seems to happen between a man and a woman now faced with the age-old question of, "Can you spend the rest of your life with this person, no regrets?"

### 8. Characters Revise Their Life Goals

At this point, the main characters have learned what they're capable of and gained that which is most precious to them. Now their life goals are revised or made anew. You can almost imagine a microphone being shoved in a character's face as someone asks, "You've done it! You've fixed all that was broken! Now what are you going to do?" This is the place to answer that question.

### 9. Possible Reemergence of the Conflict or Opposition

At the end of a book, especially in thrillers, horror novels, and mysteries, it's possible for the conflict or opposition to reemerge. The villain may rear its ugly head, implying that the conflict is about to happen all over again—just when you and the characters thought it was safe.

Remember that the reader should be left satisfied with logical resolutions to the conflicts at the end of a novel. In a truly memorable story, the reader should be reluctant to close the book despite her satisfaction.

Let's look at an example of the end section of a story evolution worksheet based on Michael Crichton's *Prey*. Notice how Crichton resolves the characters' conflicts in a satisfying way. You reluctantly close the book with a smile of relief, and a sense that good will prevail as long as there are people willing to fight for it.

STORY EVOLUTION
TITLE: *PREY*

WORKSHEET 15

**PART III: THE END**

**1. A Pivotal, Life-Changing Event Occurs**

**Detail this event and how it affects all subplots:** The main character, Jack, is trapped in a Nevada desert laboratory where an experiment has gone horribly wrong and a cloud (or swarm) of self-sustaining, self-reproducing, *intelligent* nanoparticles has escaped. Each individual nanoparticle functioning within the swarm is highly intelligent. Since the swarm was programmed to be a predator, it's becoming more deadly; if it's allowed to continue, the world will become its prey. No one outside of the laboratory even knows of the threat. By the time they realize, it'll be too late to save anyone. Unfortunately, Jack's wife, Julia, is one of the scientists who created this monstrosity. In the horrifying first scene of the end section of the book, Jack believes his wife is dead, only to see the particles of the swarm inside her putting itself back together in human form. Jack realizes that Julia has become one of the predators.

## 2. Characters Modify Short-Term Goals One Last Time

**Character 1:** Jack

**Briefly describe his final short-term goal and how he'll go about reaching it:** In the last scenes of the middle section of the book, Jack and another scientist (Mae)—the only two who haven't been taken over by the swarm—have discovered that a virus can kill the predators. Jack has to make a choice about whether to use the virus to kill his wife—who he knows is no longer the woman he loved—or to be killed by her, leaving their three children alone in the world where these predators will destroy everyone. He has to use the virus and stay alive long enough to get to the helicopter scheduled to pick them up soon.

## 3. The Showdown Begins

**Showdown details (including all main characters who are involved):** Surrounded by the predator creatures in human form, Jack throws one of the tubes containing the virus to the floor, then flees. His plan is to take the large jug containing the virus from the fabrication room, then ride the elevator to the ceiling level—where air handlers, the electrical junction boxes, and the tank for the sprinkler system are located.

The predators realize what Jack's plan is, and they go after him. Just when Jack has the open cage of the elevator in sight, he trips and goes sprawling. The jug flies from his hand. Knowing the predators are right behind him, Jack gets to his feet, grabs the jug again and runs without looking back. Unfortunately, one of the creatures is already there, standing in the elevator. Jack runs for the ladder on the wall instead. The creature in the elevator is now riding up, and Jack knows he'll be waiting for him at the top. On the ladder, Julia flies at Jack through the air, encircling his head so he can't see. Another creature has hold of his legs. Jack believes he can't go on until he thinks of his kids, and realizes he had no choice but to succeed.

With a strength he didn't know he had, Jack escapes. But as soon as he reaches the top, the other predator is waiting for him. Jack remembers the other tube of the virus in his pocket. However, the creature wraps itself in a tarp and slams into him, throwing the tube and jug from his hand. When the creature sees this, it attempts to get the jug, but Jack gets it first. Knowing what he's going to do, the predators flee the room. Jack pours the virus into the sprinkler tanks.

## 4. The Opposition Is Vanquished and the Conflict Ends

**Details:** Jack puts his lighter to the sprinkler head in the room with the predators, but the sprinklers don't come on, because the creatures have turned off the safety systems. They all jump on Jack. Suddenly there's a noise like popcorn popping. Then the tubes on a nearby machine burst open and the virus hisses out. Because the safety systems were shut off, the machine is overheating. Jack manages to get the sprinkler system to function, and the virus bursts out.

## 5. The Story Goal Is Achieved

**Detail resolution plot and all subplots:**

1. The creatures shrivel and dissolve.
2. Jack and Mae make it to the helicopter.
3. The laboratory explodes behind them.
4. Jack's children, who were exposed to the swarm, are given the virus, which cure them (although it also makes them violently ill).

### 6. Characters React to the Resolution of the Plot and Subplots

**Character 1:** Jack

**Briefly describe his reaction to the end of the conflict:** He's dead tired. He and Mae are attempting to piece together exactly what happened while the Army is acting dumb about the situation. Mae comes to tell him the good news that the virus worked, and the predators are gone. There is peace.

### 7. The *Relationship* Black Moment Is Addressed

Not applicable, as this story isn't a romance.

### 8. Characters Revise Their Life Goals

**Character 1:** Jack

**Briefly describe his life goal:** Jack realizes Julia and the scientists who released the swarm believed they had nothing to lose by doing so, but in the end they lost everything—the company, their families, their very lives. They had no understanding of what they were doing, and Jack has the e-mail trail to prove Julia's liability. Jack doesn't want such thinking to be the end of the human race. He's determined to do his part in making sure that isn't the case.

### 9. Possible Reemergence of the Conflict or Opposition

Not applicable.

Using a story evolution worksheet to plot the course of your story before spending days, weeks, or even months writing helps you to: (1) see a snapshot of the highlights of your story; (2) pinpoint with accuracy precisely where potential problems are within the story; (3) make the weak areas of your story more solid; (4) avoid sagging, uninteresting middles; and (5) avoid redundancies and repetition in your stories.

Once you've learned to see the framework of a story, you'll never look at a book the same way again. Some of you may even feel the magic has gone out of storytelling. What was invisible has become visible, even stark. But you'll now be free to embark on a journey of discovery—to see how each author went through the process of evolving her story. Think of this process as akin to deconstructing the mysteries of a whodunit. As an author yourself, you now hold the key to creating the strongest framework for your novels.

*In the next chapter, we'll begin Stage 4 of the 30-day method. We'll piece together your formatted outline in logical order, scene by scene.*

# CHAPTER 5

# Days 16–24: Your Formatted Outline

As you now know, putting together an outline is much like putting together a puzzle, except in this case you're not only assembling the pieces—you're *creating* them. You've already created several of your puzzle pieces by brainstorming, completing a preliminary outline, doing your necessary research, and filling out the three-part story evolution worksheet. In this chapter, you're going to create a formatted outline and learn how to navigate it. We'll also discuss what to do if you get stuck anywhere in the process.

The formatted outline will be the *first* draft of your novel. Once you finish the formatted outline, you'll be ready to begin your *second* (and perhaps even final) draft, which involves putting your completed outline into book form. If this sounds confusing, don't worry—you'll see what I mean once you get to that point in the process.

Right now, let's refresh ourselves on what the upcoming nine days of the 30-day schedule entail and what you'll be striving to accomplish each day.

**Stage 4: Formatted Outline**

| Schedule | What to Complete |
|---|---|
| Day 16 | Using the formatted outline capsule worksheet, turn your preliminary outline (including the summary outline and plot and character sketches), your miscellaneous scene notes, and your closing scene notes into a scene-by-scene formatted outline. |
| Day 17 | Incorporate story evolution worksheet information into outline. |
| Day 18 | Incorporate character and setting sketches throughout outline. |
| Day 19 | Incorporate your research into your outline. |
| Days 20–23 | Brainstorm to fill out the formatted outline based on the length and complexity of the story. |
| Day 24 | Create a day sheet and a table of contents. Then add chapter numbers and print out your outline. Finally, go over the hard copy, layering and strengthening the story. |

Total: 9 days to a complete formatted outline

# CONSOLIDATING YOUR INFORMATION

The primary goal of Stage 4 in the 30-day method is to consolidate all of the information you've worked so hard to develop thus far. Combining all your outline information from several different worksheets into a single document has a number of benefits:

- Because you're still working on your outline, the process of consolidating all your research, character and setting sketches, etc., into one main document will help you flesh out your outline even further. During this consolidation process, you'll be able to see the holes in your plot. You'll know in a glance what still needs work, where the pacing is slow, where you need to drop in a clue or increase the tension. You can list all your questions and issues that need further attention in the "Questions" section of the formatted outline for easy reference as you work your way through.
- Going over the outline scene-for-scene as the story progresses will help encourage your mind to brainstorm and your creativity to snowball. My writing partner, Chris Spindler, describes this as a "marvelous one-thing-leads-to-another effect that speeds up the whole creative process."
- You'll provide yourself with a snapshot of the entire book—a snapshot you can revise and fine-tune as much as you need to before you start writing. We'll talk more about revising the outline in chapter seven.

Many writers tend to get sidetracked by small details. Having everything you need in one place will help you stay focused when you start to actually write the book. You won't have to interrupt the flow of your writing to find the information you need as you work on a particular scene. Now that you know the logic behind Stage 4, let's get started.

## Outlining Tips

Outlining can and will be messy at times, regardless of how organized you are throughout the process. Here are some quick tips to help you stay on track:

- You may find it easier to complete the formatted outline capsules using a computer, since this will allow you to copy and paste information from other worksheets (if they were also completed using a computer). Typing the capsules also allows you to allot for additional space, as you'll be going back over each capsule and expanding on it throughout this stage. By typing the information now, you won't have to retype it later when you finally take everything out of outline form and put it into your second draft. If you prefer to write out your information by hand, that's perfectly fine, but remember to leave yourself plenty of space for expanding.

- Chapter numbers will change often. For now, in the earliest stage of creating a formatted outline, it's best just to divide your book into scenes (scene 1, scene 2, scene 3, etc.). Once the outline is complete or nearly complete and isn't likely to change much, you can add the specific chapter numbers.
- When you're working on a computer, it's important to insert a page break after each scene capsule. Regardless of how much (or how little) is on each page, put hard page breaks in after each scene. Most scenes will ultimately have at least a page of scene draft, possibly several pages. Some will have only a few lines, and some may even be blank. If you're unsure if there should be another scene, start a new capsule on a new page just in case. At this point in the outlining, it's fine to do this. The page break after each scene will help you to know what still needs to be done in the outline. You can always come back to it later. If you're writing by hand, start each new scene capsule on a fresh piece of paper and allow space for expansion.
- It's fine to switch between past and present tenses at this early stage. You're the only person who will see your outline.
- Sentences can be incomplete or even written in shorthand (4 = for; s/w = somewhere; w/ = with; & = and; etc.).
- Outlines do *not* need good transitions between paragraphs. Your outline will skip from subject to subject, sometimes randomly by all appearances, and that's fine. You'll smooth out rough edges during the actual writing of the novel.
- *Do* look for roughness in the logical progression of events in the outline. If the progress slows or halts in one or more scenes, it may be a signal that a scene should be placed elsewhere or taken out altogether. As long as everything is clear to you and progress is steady in your outline, go with it.
- Use description, dialogue, introspection, and action within your outline. Flesh out the outline in as much detail as possible, because it'll make the writing of the book go that much more smoothly.
- The outline must include the information you want to impart in each scene—but it doesn't have to include it eloquently. In fact, you can just write yourself notes like, "Hey, this needs to have major tension," or "Don't forget that the killer/her lover is waiting on the other side of the door!"
- Never stop viewing your outline and your story as flexible. My outlines can change slightly or drastically while I'm working on them, and sometimes even while I'm writing the book. That's how I know the magical element is turned on.

# DAY 16: STARTING AND ORGANIZING YOUR FORMATTED OUTLINE

By now, your project folder includes the following:

- in-depth character sketches
- setting sketches
- a plot sketch
- a summary outline
- miscellaneous scene notes
- closing scene notes
- all or most of the completed research from your research list
- an interview question list
- the appropriate outline aid worksheets
- a story evolution worksheet

Using all of these, you can begin piecing together your formatted outline in a logical order, scene by scene.

## Formatted Outline Capsules

The first step in combining all your information is to complete a formatted outline capsule (Worksheet 16 in Appendix C) for each scene. These brief scene summaries help you organize your information scene by scene and allow you to start thinking about all your information in an organized, linear manner. A formatted outline capsule includes the following information:

- the day the scene takes place in the story
- the chapter and scene number
- the point-of-view (POV) character
- additional characters in the scene
- the location where the scene takes place (the setting)
- the approximate time of day
- the facts necessary for writing the scene
- notes
- questions
- a draft of the scene

Let's go over these categories so that you have a clear understanding of what to include in each space. Keep in mind that if you're not sure about a particular detail, such as who the point-of-view character will be or at what time of day the scene will take place, you can put a question mark in that area for now:

## Day

The day or date will affect many aspects of the scene, so it's important to be certain of this fact, even if it's only for your own use. Consistency is very important in every novel. Keeping track of the day each scene takes place becomes extremely important when your book may eventually reach 60,000 to 100,000-plus words. Jot down either a specific date or just the day the scene takes place.

## Chapter and Scene

One chapter may contain many scenes, although some authors write very brief chapters containing only one scene each. The end of a scene within a chapter is usually indicated by several blank lines or a series of asterisks. These visual indicators tell the reader that one scene has ended and a new one is beginning.

In this section of the formatted outline capsule, you would include the chapter number and the scene number within that chapter: "chapter 4, scene 3" for instance. Initially, I suggest you skip the chapter number and simply number the scenes in order—"scene 1" for the first scene, "scene 2" for the second, and so forth. We'll talk more about this soon.

## Point-of-View (POV) Character

Who's the main character in this scene? While some writers hop from one head to the next in any given scene, very few authors can do this effectively and without annoying their readers. One character POV per scene is the best option in nearly every case. You just need the first name, or first and last name if you prefer.

## Additional Characters

List any other important characters who are in this particular scene.

## Location

Where exactly does the scene take place? You can put a location without specifics, or you can put the location and details about that location here.

## Approximate Time

What is the approximate time of day when the scene takes place? The time, like the day or date, will affect many aspects of the scene; it's important to be certain of this fact, even if it's only for your own use.

## Facts Necessary

What information is important for you to know while you draft this scene? Generally this section will include facts or research that you need to be aware of as the author, but that the reader doesn't need to know. Any of the information from the additional outline aid worksheets you filled out in chapter three (including dialogue, fact, timeline, and alibi worksheets) would fit in this section.

### Notes

This is the place to include research notes and any additional notes that pertain to another place or event within the outline, etc. If you've done an in-depth background timeline (discussed in chapter three)—you might reference it here.

In the case that you have way too much information to fit into the formatted outline document, you might want to record in this section a reference to the exact location of the information in your research notes or other document.

### Questions

If you need to figure something out before you can write a scene—for instance, you need to do more research on specific details or plot points—you can leave yourself a question or reminder in this area.

### Draft of Scene

This section will include a sketch of what happens in this scene. You may not be able to put much in this section on your first pass, but ultimately you will flesh it out fully with description, dialogue, introspection, and action—as well as your plot sketch threads and story evolution elements.

Your initial pass at a formatted outline capsule might look something like this example based on my novel *Sweet Dreams*.

FORMATTED OUTLINE CAPSULE
TITLE: *SWEET DREAMS*

| | |
|---:|:---|
| **Day:** | December 12th |
| **Chapter and Scene:** | prologue |
| **POV Character:** | Maddie |
| **Additional Characters:** | the villain (in psychic connection) |
| **Location:** | Maddie's bedroom |
| **Approximate Time:** | 7 A.M. in Wisconsin, 5 A.M. in California |
| **Facts Necessary:** | Natas Sevil is being transferred in an armored van from prison to prison. |
| **Notes:** | |
| **Questions:** | |
| **Draft of Scene:** | Maddie is alone in her bedroom when the villain comes to her via their psychic connection; he warns her that he's coming for her. |

# Incorporating Your Summary Outline Into Your Formatted Outline

Once you've finished filling out as much information for the capsules as possible, it's time to start incorporating information from other worksheets.

It's a good idea to have a copy of your summary outline created on Days 4 and 5 on hand as you work to incorporate it within the formatted outline. This way, you can check off the areas you've used as you go along, and you'll know when the scenes are all in place.

When you put the events from your summary outline into the formatted outline document, work chronologically and go as far as you can. If you're not sure about a scene, how many you should have, or what should go into a scene or scenes, insert a blank capsule, start a new capsule on the page after that, and keep going.

Page 37 of chapter two looks at an example of a summary outline using Dennis Lehane's *Mystic River*. Here's how we'd begin incorporating the information into the appropriate scene capsule.

FORMATTED OUTLINE CAPSULES
(WITH SUMMARY OUTLINE NOTES)
TITLE: *MYSTIC RIVER*

**16** WORKSHEET

**Day:** ?, 1976

**Chapter and Scene:** chapter 1, scene 1

**POV Character:** written in an omnipresent POV concerning the three boys: Sean, Jimmy, and Dave

**Additional Characters:**

**Location:** East Buckingham, specifically deals with the Point, where Sean lives, and the Flats, where Jimmy and Dave live

**Approximate Time:**

**Facts Necessary:**

**Notes:**

**Questions:**

**Draft of Scene:** Setting the scene for the focus of the book, the first part deals with how the main characters—Sean Devine, Jimmy Marcus, and Dave Boyle—became friends. Sean's and Jimmy's fathers both worked at Coleman Candy plant. Dave lived near Jimmy. They all lived in East Buckingham. Sean was from "the Point," which was "working class, blue collar, Chevys and Fords and Dodges parked in front of simple A-frames and the occasional small Victorian." In the Point, people owned their homes. In the Flats, where Jimmy and Dave lived, people rented. Sean went to school at Saint Mike's Parochial in suits and ties. Jimmy and Dave went to Lewis M. Dewey School in street clothes. If not for their fathers, they might not have been friends.

A memory of the time Jimmy jumped down on the tracks at South Station to get their errant hockey ball. People on the platform went nuts. At the last moment, several people pull Jimmy out of harm's way. Jimmy isn't bothered by any of this, but Dave throws up in his own hands and Sean looks away.

*[page break for new capsule]*

**Day:** same day

**Chapter and Scene:** chapter 1, scene 2

**POV Character:** Sean

**Additional Characters:** Sean's father

**Location:** basement tool room, where Sean's father builds birdhouses and shelves

**Approximate Time:** later that night

**Facts Necessary:**

**Notes:**

**Questions:**

**Draft of Scene:** Because of what happened at South Station earlier that day, Sean's father tells him he can't play at Jimmy's house anymore. He has to stay in view of his own house. Jimmy is simply too wild, making him a bad influence on Sean.

## Incorporating Your Miscellaneous Scene Notes

Once your summary outline is completely incorporated into the formatted outline, get out a copy of your miscellaneous scene notes (or pull up the file on your computer) that you created on Day 6.

Incorporating scenes based on your miscellaneous scene notes will be a bit harder because many times you won't be sure where they should go, or even *if* they should go. Make a guess where you think certain events might go—toward the beginning, middle, or end? Near other events already in your formatted outline? You'll be able to switch the order of the scenes easily later, so don't worry too much about putting scenes from your miscellaneous notes in exactly the right place.

If you're not sure the scene belongs in the book at all, you can either leave it out (highlighting it on your hard copy so you can come back and evaluate its worthiness later), or you can put it in wherever it seems to belong for now. Because you won't necessarily be incorporating scenes in order during this step, it may be easiest to put a question mark next to the scene number field in the outline capsule.

On pages 38–39 of chapter two, we looked at miscellaneous scene notes based on *Tom Clancy's Op-Center*. Let's revisit that example here and see how it might have translated into formatted outline capsules if the author had used this method to outline beforehand. Notice that two of the capsules contain additional details not present in the miscellaneous notes, and one capsule is still empty, leaving the possibilities open.

FORMATTED OUTLINE CAPSULES
(WITH MISCELLANEOUS SCENE NOTES)
TITLE: *TOM CLANCY'S OP-CENTER*

**Day:** Tuesday

**Chapter and Scene:** chapter 25

**POV Character:** Operations Support Officer Matt Stoll

**Additional Characters:** Paul Hood (Director) and Lowell Coffey

**Location:** Op-Center

**Approximate Time:** 7:35 A.M.

**Facts Necessary:**

**Notes:**

**Questions:**

**Draft of Scene:** Op Center computers go down, not based on a main power failure. It's impossible to bring the system down from the outside. Since the computer system is self-contained, shutdown has to come from a software command issued from inside. Matt is frantically trying to figure out what happened when the system unexpectedly comes back on—instructed by someone within to do so. The director, Lowell, and Matt realize there may be a mole inside Op-Center. At the same time that their system went down, so did portions of Defense, CIA—everywhere that the Op-Center supplies data

*[page break for new capsule]*

**Day:**

**Chapter and Scene:**

**POV Character:**

**Additional Characters:**

**Location:**

**Approximate Time:**

**Facts Necessary:**

**Notes:**

**Questions:**

**Draft of Scene:** Other scenes needed here?

*[page break for new capsule]*

| Day: | Tuesday |
|---|---|
| **Chapter and Scene:** | chapter 30 |
| **POV Character:** | Bob Herbert |
| **Additional Characters:** | Matt Stoll and Paul Hood |
| **Location:** | Op-Center |
| **Approximate Time:** | 8:05 A.M. |
| **Facts Necessary:** | |
| **Notes:** | |
| **Questions:** | |
| **Draft of Scene:** | Bob Herbert and Matt Stoll are looking at photos of Pyonyang from the National Reconnaissance Office (NRO). The photos reveal that three mechanized brigades are moving south from the North Korean capital, with four AA guns around the southern perimeter—deploying because they believe the U.S. government will be attacking. Bob and Matt report this to Director Hood. A striker team is sent. The President will have to decide how to react, and what he does will affect the outcome. War seems to be inevitable. |

*[page break for new capsule]*

## Incorporating Closing Scene Notes

Once you have all or most of your miscellaneous scene notes checked off, get out a copy of your closing scene notes, also created on Day 6.

Incorporating closing scenes won't be as hard as including miscellaneous scenes because most of them will fall in the last section of the book, and therefore you'll just put them at the end of your document in the appropriate order. If you're not sure on the order, you'll be able to switch scenes around later.

On page 39 of chapter two, we also looked at an example of a closing scene note based on the Wilson Rawls classic *Where the Red Fern Grows*. Let's see what that example would like as a formatted outline capsule. Keep in mind that we can't know what the author was thinking in the preliminary stages of working on the book, so all of this is speculation for the sake of example.

# FORMATTED OUTLINE CAPSULE
## (WITH CLOSING SCENE NOTES)
### TITLE: *WHERE THE RED FERN GROWS*

| | |
|---|---|
| **Day:** | ? |
| **Chapter and Scene:** | XIX |
| **POV Character:** | Billy Colman |
| **Additional Characters:** | his coon dogs, Old Dan and Little Ann, Billy's family |
| **Location:** | Cyclone Timber Country, and later, Billy's home in the Ozark Mountains |
| **Approximate Time:** | night |
| **Facts Necessary:** | |
| **Notes:** | |
| **Questions:** | |
| **Draft of Scene:** | During one of the end chapters, Billy goes hunting in Cyclone Timber Country with his dogs. Old Dan and Little Ann strike a trail and tree an animal right away. Little Ann whines in an unusual way that lets Billy know something is wrong. Billy is scared when Old Dan uses a low, deep, rumbling growl. He knows Old Dan won't leave the tree for anything. Billy sees they've treed a mountain lion. The lion springs at Old Dan from the tree. Little Ann joins the brutal fight, and then Billy charges in with his axe. The lion turns on Billy, but his dogs get between them. Billy sinks his axe into the eye of the lion. He faints when the lion falls toward him. |
| | When Billy comes to, his dogs finally loosen their death-grip on the lion. Old Dan is a bloody mess. As they start home, Old Dan's entrails fall out and get tangled in a bush. Billy takes Old Dan home, and his mother sews him up. Knowing he's dying, Old Dan opens his eyes and looks at Billy, giving a last sigh and a thump of his tail before closing his eyes forever. |
| | Instead of sleeping in the doghouse, Little Ann sleeps by Old Dan's lifeless body on the porch that night. Billy buries Old Dan the next morning by the foot of a red oak tree. |
| | The life goes out of Little Ann without her brother, and Billy finds her one morning on Old Dan's grave—dead. |

At the end of Day 16, your outline should be shaping up very nicely. You will have incorporated your summary outline notes, miscellaneous scene notes, and closing scene notes within the formatted outline document. Now take a look at the outline from top to bottom. You'll see a lot of holes, but you'll also see a solid progression.

Each scene you write has to advance the story. Every scene must add to the one before and work to move the plot forward. Your formatted outline acts as a road map: You can see the path you must take, and you can place your scenes accordingly. It's much easier to pace your novel when it's in outline form than it would be if you just started writing the story. With an outline sketching out each scene in detail, you can tell at a glance or two whether each scene pushes the plot to a tight conclusion. Once you complete the formatted outline, any scene that seems to slow or halt progress—or that simply doesn't belong—can be moved or cut before the actual writing of the book begins.

With the beginning of your formatted outline together, you should now have a good idea where the story needs work. If you can, work on filling in those holes for the rest of this day. If the snowball effect begins, go with it. Piece together and flesh out the outline as much as possible. Snowballing is a miracle that should never be stopped once it starts.

Once you've gone as far as you can for the day, number the pages in the formatted outline document, then print it. You've now provided yourself with a one-glance method of knowing exactly which scenes need further fleshing out. You can make as many hand-written notes on this hard copy as you want. During this stage of the 30-day process, you'll be adding notes as you go and reprinting the outline each day.

## The "Pick Up the Pace" Ploy

If you want to pick up the pace of your book in a simple way your readers probably won't even notice on a conscious level, try writing one scene per chapter. This accomplishes several things.

- Fairly short chapters allow the book to move along swiftly from one chapter to the next.
- Your reader is likely to read more in one sitting, since many readers glance ahead to the next chapter when considering whether or not to stop reading. If the next chapter is short, they'll be much more inclined to read "just one more" chapter. Frequently, they won't put the book down for several more short chapters.
- Your reviews are more likely to include comments like "page-turner," "nail-biter," and "couldn't put it down."

You can also follow Tracy Chevalier's example in *Girl With the Pearl Earring*. There are no chapters. The book is divided into four parts, each based on a year in the life of Griet, the main character. Each scene within those parts is very short—in most cases no more than a page or two—and scenes are divided with a fancy curlicue. I read the book in one sitting, in less than seven hours. The short scenes flew, always leaving me panting for more.

Try this ploy on your next novel to see if it makes a difference in your pacing—possibly even in the reviews you receive for it.

You've done a tremendous amount of work today, but if your mind is anything like mine, you won't be able to stop yourself from brainstorming for the rest of the day. If that happens to you, it's working! If it doesn't, no worries. Let yourself relax. We've still got a lot of work ahead of us.

# DAY 17: INCORPORATING STORY EVOLUTION ELEMENTS

On Day 17 of the 30-day method, you'll be incorporating the elements from your story evolution worksheet into your formatted outline, which was created on Days 14 and 15. Your story evolution worksheet is in chronological order, so figuring out where the events on this worksheet fit into your outline shouldn't be too difficult.

On pages 65–68 of chapter four, we looked at a sample story evolution worksheet based on J.R.R. Tolkien's *The Fellowship of the Ring*. Here's a portion of that example to refresh your memory.

STORY EVOLUTION WORKSHEET
TITLE: *THE FELLOWSHIP OF THE RING*

**PART II: THE MIDDLE**

**3. First Short Term Goals Are Thwarted**

**Briefly detail the events that take place:** On the road, Black Riders are searching for the Ring. They pursue the companions. When they escape the Black Riders, there's a letter from Gandalf at The Prancing Pony, telling them that a ranger, Strider, will lead them to Rivendell, and that Gandalf will join them when he can. During the next leg of the journey, when Frodo puts the Ring on, the Black Riders are alerted to him and surround the travelers. Frodo is stabbed by the Black Rider King's knife.

15
WORKSHEET

Now, let's see how that example translates into a scene capsule.

FORMATTED OUTLINE CAPSULE
(WITH STORY EVOLUTION NOTES)
TITLE: *THE FELLOWSHIP OF THE RING*

**Day:** ?

**Chapter and Scene:** chapter XI, scene 9

**POV Character:** book is written with an omnipresent POV (or from all viewpoints at the same time)

**Additional Characters:** Sam, Pippin, Strider, Frodo, Merry, Black Riders

**Location:** Weathertop

**Approximate Time:** late day

**Facts Necessary:**

**Notes:**

**Questions:**

**Draft of Scene:** The group sees signs that rangers (and, likely, Gandalf) may have come before them in this place but had to flee because of the Dark Riders. Strider tells the group about the Black Riders—elven kings of old who have become shadow wraiths after falling under the power of the Ring.

The group lights a fire to keep the shadow wraiths back, but they come anyway, desperately drawn by the Ring, and surround the group.

Frodo's terror temps him to put on the Ring. He sees the shadow wraiths in the spirit world, and one of them springs forward and stabs Frodo with his knife. Frodo removes the Ring.

Incorporate as much of your story evolution elements into your formatted outline as you can. If you're not sure about something, highlight that area on the hard copy of your story evolution worksheet so you can come back to it later.

At the end of Day 17, take another look at your outline from top to bottom. Flesh out the outline wherever you can. Once you've gone as far as you can for the day, print it. Spend the rest of the day looking at it, trying to fill in the holes.

# DAY 18: INCORPORATING CHARACTER AND SETTING SKETCHES

On Day 18 of the 30-day method, you'll be incorporating your character sketches directly into the formatted outline.

In the preliminary outline, you didn't need to worry about how and where you put character information into the outline. You just filled out the worksheets. But, as you're putting together the formatted outline, you need to think about how and where you need to incorporate character sketch information. Up to this point, you've been putting scenes in chronological order. Incorporating a character sketch isn't as easy as dropping a scene into its chronological place, so today's tasks will be a bit trickier for you. However, because much of your outline is now in a progressive (or linear) format, you should be able to determine the best places to intersperse your character sketch information.

Remember as you work that, in general, most character sketch information will appear in the beginning of the book, when the character is first introduced. As you introduce your characters and they begin to interact with one another, drop in short physical descriptions. Include some information about their personalities and motivations in every scene. Writing sensory descriptions of your characters and their behavior gives your readers the ability to move and use their senses right along with your characters. Put these descriptions directly in your outline.

Blocks of description are fine in the outline. Don't worry about being eloquent in delivering the description. When you're writing the book, you can scatter the information throughout several scenes, wherever it seems to fit best, in creative ways that tie together naturally.

I've always been sparse when it comes to descriptions. I dislike writing them, and I dislike reading them. I prefer to include just a couple of interesting sentences to get the reader's own imagination going. Because my descriptions are generally short, it's simple for me to cut and paste a paragraph or two describing each character into various scenes, where it makes the most sense in the outline. I usually place these character descriptions in the first five or so scenes of the book, where I most need the information for setup. I put this information in *each* of those opening scenes and anywhere else I think I might need it. Then I don't have to go on an all-out search for it when it comes time to write that scene.

Ask yourself some or all of the questions below as you're incorporating character sketch information into your formatted outline:

- What are the characters seeing, touching, smelling, hearing, and tasting?
- What are they wearing, and how does their clothing affect the other person(s) in the scene?
- Where are they within the scene? Is there anything near them that holds meaning to them, and if so, what and why?
- What are their expressions? Do they seem nervous, emotional, guarded?
- What is happening around them? What is the POV character's reaction to the event(s)?
- What are they thinking?
- If there are other characters in the scene, does the POV character know them? If he does, how does this relationship affect him?

At this point, start adding dialogue to your formatted outline as well. Dialogue advances and enriches a scene, and, in your finished story, provides the reader with a sense of "being there." Use both external dialogue (what characters say out loud) and internal monologue (what the main POV character in the scene thinks to himself). Dialogue can also be used to reveal important details about a character's personality. It can be used to start a scene with a bang, and it will paint a clearer picture in your mind of the purpose of the scene.

Let's take a look at an example of how character sketch information can be interspersed into a scene capsule. We'll start with this sample character sketch worksheet based on Philip K. Dick's *The Minority Report*.

## CHARACTER SKETCH
## TITLE: *THE MINORITY REPORT*

**Character Name:** General Leopold Kaplan
**Nickname:**
**Birth Date/Place:**
**Character Role:** villain

**PHYSICAL DESCRIPTIONS**
**Age:** 70 or older
**Race:** white
**Eye Color:** ?, but wears rimless glasses for reading
**Hair Color/Style:** little hair, dusty brown
**Build (Height/Weight):** thin, wiry
**Skin Tone:** pale
**Style of Dress:** vest, gold pocket watch, silver cane, conservative business suit; as General Kaplan, wears his service bars, medals, boots and gloves, decorative short-sword and visored cap

**Characteristics/
Mannerisms:** nervousness

**PERSONALITY TRAITS:**

**BACKGROUND:** After the Angelo-Chinese War, the AFWA (Army of the Federated Westbloc Alliance) was demilitarized and the officers were forced to retire and were discarded.

**INTERNAL CONFLICTS:** Wants to shut down the Precrime system by proving it is contaminated, which will cause it to be discredited and abolished by the Army. Then the AFWA will run the complete show, doing their own police work the way they used to.

**EXTERNAL CONFLICTS:** Because of the majority report generated from two of the precogs says that John Anderton, the founder and Precrime Commissioner, will kill him, Kaplan risks his own life by continuing to try to abolish the Precrime system.

**OCCUPATION/
EDUCATION:** Kaplan is a retired general of the AFWA. He also heads the Veterans' League, an exclusive organization of high-ranking officers of international classes from both sides of the war.

Here's how this information can be incorporated into a scene capsule.

## FORMATTED OUTLINE CAPSULE
## (WITH CHARACTER SKETCH NOTES)
## TITLE: *THE MINORITY REPORT*

|  |  |
|---|---|
| **Day:** | ? |
| **Chapter and Scene:** | chapter IX |
| **POV Character:** | John Anderton, Precrime founder and Commissioner |
| **Additional Characters:** | former AFWA and Veterans' League members; General Leopold Kaplan; police units; the Army; a crowd of citizens |
| **Location:** | army rally |
| **Approximate Time:** | ? |
| **Facts Necessary:** | After the Angelo-Chinese War, the Army of the Federated Westbloc Alliance (AFWA) was demilitarized and the officers were forced to retire and were discarded. Kaplan is a retired general of the AFWA. He also heads the Veterans' League, an exclusive organization of high-ranking officers of international classes from both sides of the war. A nervous man, Kaplan is about 70 years old, thin, wiry, and pale. He wears glasses for reading. For this occasion, he's forgone his conservative business suit and wears his service bars, medals, boots and gloves, decorative short-sword, and visored cap. |
| **Notes:** | |
| **Questions:** | |
| **Draft of Scene:** | Anderton arrives at the Army rally in a police car. Kaplan is surprised to see him, since what he has to say to the surging masses will discredit the Precrime Agency and eventually make it obsolete—the way the AFWA was made obsolete after the Angelo-Chinese War. Anderton knows Kaplan wants to prove the Precrime system is contaminated and, therefore, cause it to be discredited and abolished by the Army. Then the AFWA will run the show, doing their own police work the way they used to. |
|  | Kaplan reveals the contamination of the Precrime system, which sends to detention camps men and women accused of crimes they haven't yet committed (but *will* commit) based on the precognitive information obtained in the form of majority and minority reports generated at the Precrime Agency. The first two precogs asserted in the majority report that Anderton would murder Kaplan. However, the minority report from the third precog invalidated the majority report, causing Kaplan to mistakenly believe Anderton won't kill him. Anderton has reasoned that the only way to keep Kaplan from destroying the Precrime system is by fulfilling the publicized majority report, which stated that Anderton does kill Kaplan. |

Now it's time to incorporate your setting sketches and any setting-specific research directly into the formatted outline. Much of the discussion pertaining to incorporating character sketch information into your formatted outline also applies to the incorporation of setting sketches. Most of the important setting sketches will come at the beginning of the book, when the setting is first introduced, but you'll also establish setting for the reader with every new scene. Include all necessary information in each scene in the outline. For instance, if you introduce your hero's home in the first scene, that would be a good place to drop in a short description of his abode. As with the character sketches, put your setting information *wherever you might need it* within the formatted outline, so you won't have to hunt for it when it comes time to write that scene.

Ask yourself some or all of the following questions as you incorporate setting sketch information into your formatted outline:

- What about the setting is important? Characters will notice things that are important to them or that hold special meaning for them. Their current state of mind will also affect what they notice.
- What season is it? What kind of day within that season? Rainy? Hot? How does your character react to the weather?
- Where are the characters within the scene?
- Does your setting description match the mood of the scene?

Just as you did with the character sketch information, give your readers sensory descriptions—allow them to feel the wind or cold darkness of a damp night.

Let's take a look at an example of a setting sketch information as it would be included in a scene capsule. We'll start with a sample general setting sketch worksheet based on Tracy Chevalier's *Girl With a Pearl Earring*.

### GENERAL SETTING SKETCH
### TITLE: *GIRL WITH A PEARL EARRING*

| | |
|---|---|
| **Name of Setting:** | Delft |
| **Characters Living in Region/Time Period:** | Griet |
| **Year or Time Period:** | 1664–1676 (17th century) |
| **Season:** | multiple |
| **City and State:** | Delft, the Netherlands |
| **Miscellaneous Notes:** | See corresponding Worksheet 2B for details. |

Now let's look at a character setting sketch for Griet.

## CHARACTER SETTING SKETCH
### TITLE: *GIRL WITH A PEARL EARRING*

**Character Name:** Griet

**General Settings to Include:** See corresponding Worksheet 2A for details.

**CHARACTER'S HOME SURROUNDINGS:**

**City or Town:** Delft (See corresponding Worksheet 2A for more details.)

**Neighborhood:** unspecified

**Street:** canal runs along side street

**Neighbors:** unspecified

**Home:** narrow brick house with a steep roof

**Home Interior:** unspecified

**CHARACTER'S WORKPLACE:** Griet is sent to work in the painter Vermeer's home as a maid.

**City or Town of Workplace:** Papists' Corner

**Business Name:** not applicable

**Type of Business:** not applicable

**Neighborhood:** After crossing a bridge over the canal, there's the Market Square, where horses and carts clatter over the stones. On the right, there's the Town Hall with a gilded front and white marble. To the left, there's the New Church with a tall, narrow tower. In the center of the Square, the stones are laid to form an 8-pointed star set inside a circle.

**Street:** on the Oude Langendijck, where it intersects with the Molenpoort

**Individual Workspace:** Griet is to clean Vermeer's studio: There's a scent of linseed oil in the large, square room with white-washed walls, and there are gray and white marble tiles on the floor with darker tiles set in the pattern of square crosses. Very little furniture. The easel and a chair are set in front of the middle window with a table placed in front of the window in the right corner. On the far wall, there's a cupboard with brushes, palette knives, and clean palettes. In the far corner, opposite the table and window, there's a storeroom.

**Co-workers:** Tanneke

**MISCELLANEOUS NOTES:** Vermeer's end house, with the Molenpoort running down one side so it's a little wider than the other houses on the street, is grand with two stories and an attic. The ground-floor windows are very high. On the first floor, there are three windows set close together.

Now we'll incorporate this information into a formatted outline capsule.

**FORMATTED OUTLINE CAPSULE
(WITH SETTING SKETCH NOTES)
TITLE: *GIRL WITH A PEARL EARRING***

| | |
|---:|:---|
| **Day:** | Griet's second day working for the Vermeers |
| **Chapter and Scene:** | ? |
| **POV Character:** | Griet |
| **Additional Characters:** | Catharina (Vermeer's wife) and Maria Thins (Catharina's mother) |
| **Location:** | Vermeer's studio |
| **Approximate Time:** | early morning |
| **Facts Necessary:** | Description of Vermeer's studio: There's a scent of linseed oil in the large, square room with white-washed walls, gray and white marble tiles on the floor with darker tiles set in the pattern of square crosses. Very little furniture. The easel and a chair are set in front of the middle window, with a table placed in front of the window in the right corner. On the far wall, there's a cupboard with brushes, palette knives, and clean palettes. In the far corner, opposite the table and window, there's a storeroom. |
| **Notes:** | In addition to a description of Vermeer's studio, this scene includes a detailed description of an actual painting done by Vermeer of van Ruijven's wife. More detailed notes on these may be included elsewhere. |
| **Questions:** | |
| **Draft of Scene:** | Catharina unlocks her husband's studio door and instructs Griet on how to clean the room. Griet knows she must clean it thoroughly without seeming to move anything. She does this by measuring with her fingers, hands, feet, knees, shoulders, and chin. She leaves the easel for last, where Vermeer's current painting-in-progress sits. Griet is utterly captured by it. Maria Thins catches her looking at it and tells her about it and Vermeer's working methods. |

At the end of Day 18, review your outline. Type out any handwritten notes and reprint your formatted outline. Spend the rest of the day looking at it, brainstorming to fill in the holes.

# DAY 19: INCORPORATING RESEARCH

On Day 19 of the 30-day method, you'll be incorporating your book research directly into the formatted outline.

If there's a fact in your research that's pertinent to a specific scene in the outline, you would incorporate it into the "Facts Necessary" section of the scene capsule. Include the fact in all the scenes where you might need it.

If you have large amounts of research that can't be incorporated into the outline without causing your page count to triple, place a reference to the research in the "Notes" section of your scene capsule so you'll know exactly where to find the information when you need it.

Putting all of this information directly into your outline will shave considerable time off your schedule when it's time to write the book. Everything you need is just *where* you need it, *when* you need it. Speaking from experience, I know how easy it is to get sidetracked into an all-out research session just to figure out exactly what kind of chair your hero's going to plant his worn-denim-clad butt on. Having everything *in the outline* eliminates that problem when it comes time to write each scene.

Let's take a look at how research notes can be included into a scene capsule. Remember that the research you're going to incorporate at this stage will probably come from several different sources, not just one worksheet (as was the case in earlier examples). The following example is based on *The Fifteenth Letter* by myself and Chris Spindler. Pay close attention to the use of the "Notes" and "Facts Necessary" sections.

---

## FORMATTED OUTLINE CAPSULES (WITH RESEARCH NOTES) TITLE: *THE FIFTEENTH LETTER*

**16 WORKSHEET**

**Date:** 15 years ago

**Chapter and Scene:** prologue

**POV Character:** Serena Salim

**Additional Characters:** Roman Salim (15 years old), Zeke Carfi, Nelson Salim (Zeke's partner in crime), a couple of police officers

**Location:** Madison; outside Eisner Bank & Trust (a fictional bank) in van, then in Nelson's house

**Approximate Time:** ?

**Facts Necessary:**

**Notes:** See map research notes [mapsresearch.doc] for specifics on the rare bookstores, specifically Nelson's shop: pages 3–4.

See background timelines [backgroundtime.doc] for specifics on Roman, Nelson, Zeke, Serena, etc.: pages 1–2, 12, 14.

**Questions:**

**Draft of Scene:** Roman (Nelson's son) is at the scene of this crime with Serena, who is Nelson's wife and Roman's mother. Roman is with his mother in the getaway van outside Eisner Bank & Trust. Someone is being rolled out of the bank on a gurney, in a body bag. Roman says out loud, "Is it a bank accountant or something?" Then Zeke comes out. Where is his dad? He's confused and demands his mother find out, but she says they have to get out of there.

At home, from another room, Serena sobs and lies to the police, saying she and her son weren't involved in the robbery. The police have seized Nelson's shop of rare books. Earlier, they saw information about the bank robbery on the news: Zeke killed Nelson. Nelson was about to shoot the bank manager, whom they had taken hostage/or who refused to tell them the combination of the safe. Zeke tried to stop Nelson with words and, when that didn't do, Zeke shot him. He only planned to shoot him in the arm, but Nelson moved suddenly and the shot killed him. Zeke has turned into a kind of hero because he saved the bank manager's life. Of course he has to serve time for planning and carrying out an armed bank robbery, but the press loves him.

Serena knows her husband was a failure in many senses of the word. He wasn't clever enough to pull off the crimes he set out to commit. Zeke was the brains behind their partnership. Serena has always known Nelson was a thief. She didn't care. She'd spent a lifetime in poverty. He promised her the moon. Now look where she is. She has nothing. Zeke has betrayed them all. What will become of her? She won't go back to being poor. She won't.

*[page break for new capsule]*

| | |
|---:|:---|
| **Date:** | Tuesday |
| **Chapter and Scene:** | chapter 1 |
| **POV Character:** | Amber Carfi (daughter of Zeke Carfi) |
| **Additional Characters:** | Warren Jensen, Gene (bank robber) |
| **Location:** | Amber and Jensen's patrol car, then at the Falcon's Bend bank, running down Main Street |
| **Approximate Time:** | just after 4 P.M. |
| **Facts Necessary:** | Full-time patrol officers schedule: |

> 1st shift: 6 A.M. to 4 P.M. (10 hour shift)
> 2nd shift: 2 P.M. to midnight (10 hour shift)
> 3rd shift: 10 P.M. to 8 A.M. (10 hour shift)

So 8 days on (Wednesday to Wednesday); 6 days off (Thursday to Tuesday), meaning everyone working full-time Wednesday; they work 40 hours a week; and they get every other weekend off. They alternate on which shift they work. So 8 days on, they work 1st shift; 6 days off, then they work 2nd shift for 8 days; 6 days off, then they work 3rd shift for 8 days; 6 days off, and they start all over again.

| | |
|---:|:---|
| **Notes:** | |
| **Questions:** | |
| **Draft of Scene:** | Jensen and Amber just got a 10-90 (bank alarm). A silent alarm (in a bank, to alert the police without alerting the robber) was called in; no confirmation from bank employees at this time. |

Amber sees Jensen grimace because they're technically off-duty, but they're closest to the bank.

Jensen asks Amber if she wants him to take primary. Amber says, "No way." She's excited.

When they arrive at the bank, Dispatch tells them they've had confirmation from the bank president; the subject went out a back exit with an unreported amount of money.

High-action chase, foot pursuit. Amber was on the track team, as well as football. She overtakes subject in black mask, tackles him. Her handheld radio goes off as she cuffs him. Jensen calls in the 10-95 (subject in custody). The robber took barely a hundred bucks. Hardly worth the effort.

Amber says something to the bank robber about crime not paying. Robber says, "How would you know?" Amber says robbing banks runs in her family.

At the end of Day 19, review your formatted outline, type in any handwritten notes, and reprint it.

## DAYS 20–23: BRAINSTORMING

On Days 20–23, you'll be brainstorming to fill out the remaining holes in your outline. You want to layer and strengthen your story. Hopefully, your work thus far has inspired you to brainstorm constantly, and your outline is coming together like a dream. As you work, you can type your notes directly into your formatted outline document or write by hand on your printed copy. Reprint the formatted outline as often as you need to during this time.

### Roadblocks

With the proper brainstorming and discipline on your part, the 30-day method should keep you outlining from start to finish. However, there may be times you'll hit a roadblock anyway. Murphy's Law—there really is no escape. So what do you do? Here's a list of ideas you can try:

1. Use any of the brainstorming techniques included in chapter one, especially verbal brainstorming with a partner. You might be able to work out the kinks and return to outlining in no time.

2. If you haven't started your research (or if you haven't finished your research), do it now, or follow another logical research angle. You might discover some new threads you can explore in your outline.

3. Remember that you don't have to brainstorm or puzzle out your outline in a linear fashion. If you can't figure out what should happen in scenes twelve through twenty, but scenes at the end of the book are coming to you, skip ahead and work

on those. In the process, you might figure out what needs to happen in scenes twelve through twenty. All that matters is that you keep brainstorming and allowing your muse to help you work.

4. If you've tried all of the suggestions above and you're still not able to move forward, take a few days off to brainstorm in your head instead of on paper. Use any of the brainstorming ideas in chapter one to light a fire under your creative coffeepot if you can. If that doesn't work, take a longer break. Give yourself permission not to take notes so you'll feel freer to go in any direction while you brainstorm.

Ultimately, if you can't get past the roadblock with any of the previous suggestions, you may need to set the project aside. Perhaps the story just isn't finished brewing. The work you've done so far will prove invaluable when you're ready to start again. For now, take some time off, do some research for another story, brainstorm on other books, or concentrate on one that's ready to be poured out. Setting a story aside for more brewing is *not* a sign of failure. You might actually discover down the road that it was a blessing.

If you believe you need to send the current project back for more brewing, carefully print everything you've done up to this point and put it all together in your project folder. Make sure you write down the file names of each document on the first page of each hard copy, so you'll know exactly where to look when you come back to it later.

If you begin an outline and can't finish it, you may still be in the muse-driven stage—the place every writer is in before she learns how to make her muse her assistant rather than her master—and need to remain there for awhile to grow as a writer. You'll still be able to use many of the suggestions in *First Draft in 30 Days* to help you learn the process of completing a novel.

## Outlining and Writing in Tandem

Many writers hit snags the first few times they try completing a formatted outline. If you find yourself unable to make further progress, the cure is almost always outlining and writing in tandem. Stop outlining, sit down, and write some scenes from the book based on your outline. This will encourage the story to take shape in your mind and will almost always inspire you toward further brainstorming, which will help you complete your formatted outline.

When outlining and writing in tandem, start by outlining as many scenes as you can. When you can't go any further, stop and use the completed portion of your formatted outline to write the first scene of the book. Once that scene is complete, try going back to the outline. If you're still stuck, write the second scene. As you push forward, eventually the story will reveal itself, allowing you to complete the outline well in advance of the book.

If you're outlining and writing in tandem, please note that you probably won't be able to follow the 30-day schedule. This method is designed around completing a full outline *before* you begin the writing, so follow your own schedule while you're doing this.

In general, once you get all your summary outline ideas, miscellaneous and closing scene notes, character and setting sketches, research, plot sketches, and story evolution worksheets incorporated into a formatted outline, your story is sufficiently complete that you can *start* writing. The first few times I used this outlining method, I hit a roadblock around chapter four and was able to move forward by writing in tandem with outlining. The rest of the outline came together as I wrote the book. In each case, the outline was complete before I finished writing half of the book. Now I'm able to finish and revise the outline before ever writing a word of the book.

Eventually you'll be able to do the same. Your goal should be to get to the point where you're able to outline a book straight through before starting to write the book itself. The reason this is so important: It's much easier to revise an outline than an entire book. You can strengthen weak areas, blot out huge blunders, and smooth out roughness *before* these flaws have spread over three hundred pages. Because your outline is, essentially, the first draft of the book, your first attempt at actually writing the book will produce your second (and possibly final) draft, which will require only minor editing and polishing when it's complete.

Each project will be a little different for you. Even if you manage to piece the entire outline together first, it may change slightly or dramatically when you start writing the book itself, and that's fine. Your outline is very flexible!

At the end of Day 23 (if you're not outlining and writing in tandem), review your formatted outline from top to bottom. You should be pretty close to filling in all the gaps in the outline at this point. Once you've gone as far as you can for the day, reprint it.

## Mystery Novels and Writing in Tandem

Writing in tandem with outlining works for most genres, but you may find it difficult if you're writing a mystery novel. Mystery novels are complicated—perhaps more complicated than any other genre of fiction. You have to juggle a lot of facts, information, characters, and details. Careful and accurate research is also a necessity.

Before you start any type of mystery novel, you should prepare with a full outline. Since your outline itself is going to require one or more revisions, it makes sense to revise the *outline* until you've got a solid plot instead of revising draft after draft.

## DAY 24: CREATING A DAY SHEET AND TABLE OF CONTENTS

If you're writing a 100,000-word book, your complete formatted outline will be nearly a hundred pages long, or longer. Even a shorter book, say 60,000 words, will require about sixty pages of outline. How do you navigate something this big and complicated?

The first step is to separate scenes with page breaks so each scene can be viewed completely on its own. Doing this will make your document far more workable. When you finish writing a scene, you'll shuffle the scene capsule to the back of the stack until you eventually end up back at the beginning of the outline. Adding a page break at the end of each scene will keep you focused on writing at least one scene per *day*, which is important to completing a project on schedule.

A day sheet (Worksheet 17 in Appendix C) is a valuable tool when you're evaluating the strength of your outline. It will also help you construct a table of contents, which will help you navigate your outline. On Day 24 in the 30-day schedule, it's time to create your day sheet and a table of contents. Your day sheet will probably run to several pages.

Look at this example of a partially completed day sheet based on J.L. Hansen's *LogOut*.

DAY SHEET
TITLE: *LOGOUT*

| Day | Chapter and Scene | POV | Total POVs for Character | High-Concept Blurb |
|-----|-------------------|-----|--------------------------|--------------------|
| **Week 2: Monday** | prologue, scene 1 | Aaron Braggonier | 1 | Aaron and his Mercedes go into the ocean. |
| **Week 1: Monday** | chapter 1, scene 1 | Julie Wynn | 1 | Corporate life is making Julie and her co-workers sick—literally. |
| **Week 1: Monday** | chapter 1, scene 2 | Julie | 2 | Julie takes her resignation letter to her boss and is offered a future promotion. |
| **Week 1: Monday** | chapter 1, scene 3 | Julie | 3 | Air Quality team is introduced. |
| **Week 1: Monday** | chapter 1, scene 4 | Logan Silva | 1 | A nervous Logan tries to contact Charles Turpin, his benefactor. |
| **Week 1: Monday** | chapter 1, scene 5 | Charles Turpin | 1 | Turpin agrees to meet Logan. |

WORKSHEET 17

| Day | Chapter and Scene | POV | Total POVs for Character | High-Concept Blurb |
|---|---|---|---|---|
| **Week 1: Monday** | chapter 1, scene 6 | Logan | 2 | Logan threatens Turpin in order to get more money for their scheme; Turpin refuses. |
| **Week 1: Monday** | chapter 1, scene 7 | Julie | 4 | Julie arrives home to discover she's forgotten her brother's birthday. |
| **Week 1: Monday** | chapter 1, scene 8 | Logan | 3 | Logan reveals to his partner in crime, who lives with his family, that their ploy to get more money out of Turpin didn't work. |
| **Week 1: Tuesday** | chapter 2, scene 1 | Logan | 4 | Logan makes a reckless decision to save his dreams. |
| **Week 1: Tuesday** | chapter 2, scene 2 | Julie | 5 | Determined to solve the mystery of ExecuSource's sick employees, Julie meets Cam Clay of Air Quality, hoping to get some answers from him. |

The information in your scene capsules will help you fill out the first three columns. In the first column, insert the day the scene takes place. Enter the chapter and scene number within that chapter in column two. Then list the scene's point-of-view character in column three.

This number in column four is a running tab counting how many times, up to that scene, that a particular character has held POV. In the example above, Julie was the POV character in five of the eleven listed scenes. Keeping track of this number is especially helpful in books with more than a couple of points-of-view. In one of the books in the Falcon's Bend series, my partner and I filled out our day sheet and discovered that one of the characters had only one or two POV scenes in the entire 110,000-word book. These scenes, we realized, were extraneous or worked better from another POV.

If you find that one of your characters has only two or three POV scenes, you might want to cut the scenes or change them to another character's POV. Your readers don't want to get interested in a character who doesn't have a strong purpose throughout the book. The exception to this rule is the prologue, which can be written from a point-of-view not repeated elsewhere in the book. The technique of using a one-time POV character in the prologue is especially common in mystery and suspense novels.

Column five on the day sheet features a high-concept blurb, which is a very succinct sentence summing up what takes place in that scene. You could also look at it as a summary of something a particular character must do or wants to do. What is his short-term goal for this scene? An easy way of figuring out a high concept blurb for each of your scenes is to answer the following question:

*[Character's name]* ——————— *needs or wants to*
*[do what]* ——————— ?

The high-concept blurb is a single, tantalizing sentence that sums up the entire scene. You will use these extremely short, single sentences to sum up what happens in every scene in the book. You don't have to worry about creating a tantalizing high-concept blurb unless you want to tantalize yourself—you'll be the only person looking at this.

Day sheets have many other vital uses. In chapter eight, you'll see how the basic day sheet can be re-invented for many different, useful purposes.

## Turning Your Day Sheet Into a Table of Contents

Once you complete your day sheet, you'll be ready to create a table of contents. Although the table format of the day sheet will ultimately be very useful, a simple linear format is best for a workable table of contents. As you'll notice in the example below, the information comes directly from the day sheet—all you have to do is add the page numbers:

| From Day Sheet to Table of Contents | |
| --- | --- |
| **Week 2: Monday** | **2** |
| Prologue. Aaron (1): Aaron and his Mercedes go into the ocean | 2 |
| **Week 1: Monday** | **3** |
| Chapter One, Scene 1. Julie (1): Corporate life is making Julie and her co-workers sick—literally | 3 |
| Chapter One, Scene 2. Julie (2): Julie takes her resignation letter to her boss and is offered a future promotion | 4 |
| Chapter One, Scene 3. Julie (3): Air Quality team is introduced | 5 |

Create your table of contents as a separate document on your computer. Once it's complete, cut and paste it into your formatted outline document. If you supplement or re-arrange your outline after this point, you may need to update the table of contents to make sure the page numbers are correct. This will ensure that your table of contents remains a helpful navigation tool.

*With the formatted outline complete and a day sheet ready to go, it's time to move on to Stage 5: Outline Evaluation.*

# CHAPTER 6

# Days 25–28: Evaluating the Strength of Your Formatted Outline

Once you have a formatted outline of your book, you should be able to look at it critically to decide if the story has a solid plot with plenty of tension in all the right places. You can assess the outline to make sure everything is consistent. Is each plot thread introduced and concluded properly? Does each plot thread follow a logical, steady path to its resolution? Is your plot infused with tension? Do plot and tension lag anywhere? If there are problems, you can rework scenes until they all flow forward smoothly.

But what if you're not sure your book has everything it needs? What if you can't decide just by looking at the outline if your pacing is steady, and you don't know—even after reviewing the outline countless times—whether the threads develop and conclude in the proper way? What if you can't tell if your tension is ebbing?

You can systematically evaluate the strength of your outline by deconstructing it using a method I call tagging and tracing. Basically, tagging and tracing is *identifying* all the plot threads within the outline, then *following* them to make sure they're strong enough throughout each section of the book. Remember that each plot thread should stand on its own—when you isolate a particular thread, you should be able to see a clear progression from start to finish.

You've already completed most of the work that will enable you to perform this critical analysis of your outline. Here's the schedule for this step.

**Stage 5: Evaluate the Strength of Your Formatted Outline**

| Schedule | What to Complete |
|---|---|
| Days 25–26 | Tag and trace your threads. |
| Day 27 | Isolate each plot thread. |
| Day 28 | Revise weak elements. |

Total: 4 days to a solid, usable outline

Please note that this hands-on step is completely optional. If you're an experienced author, you may feel confident *mentally* assessing the structure in your outline. However, if you're a little unsure, the manual approach of tagging, tracing, and isolating threads may be more beneficial. If you discover weak areas in your outline, you may find it useful to revisit your story evolution worksheet (Worksheet 15 in Appendix C). If you have an editor, agent, or critique partner you trust, ask that person to read your outline to help you evaluate its strength.

There are no worksheets for the steps in this chapter simply because every story is so different. Just follow the instructions contained in each section, and you'll be able to properly evaluate the strength of your outline.

## DAYS 25–26: TAGGING AND TRACING

Start Day 25 by checking for unanswered questions on your interview questions worksheet (Worksheet 8 in Appendix C). If you still need answers to some of the questions, set up an appointment with your chosen expert. Try to schedule the appointment for Day 29 of the outlining process—at this point, you'll be putting the finishing touches on your outline.

Once that's taken care of, get out the hard copy of your plot sketch worksheet and open your formatted outline document on your computer. You'll also need the most current hard copy of your formatted outline. If you're working on your computer, I highly suggest that you save a new, separate copy of your formatted outline specifically for use during the tagging and tracing process. You're about to make your outline very messy, so be prepared.

In chapter two, you created the plot threads for your story:

- story goal
- romance thread (optional, depending on genre)
- subplot threads
- plot tension
- romantic/sexual tension (optional, depending on genre)
- release
- downtime
- black moment (in a romance novel, you'll have two black moments—one for the story goal and one for the romance thread)
- resolution
- aftereffects of resolution (optional)

All of these threads should become invisible as you write the book. If something is amiss in your structure, however, you'll see it clearly in the outline. The progression of the story may come to a stop, or the pacing, tension, or conflict may seem to sag.

Pacing is the steady progression of your unfolding plot. Genre dictates pacing, in some part. A coming-of-age story or an angst-driven romance will have a much slower pace than an action-adventure or mystery novel. Nevertheless, *all* stories need consistent development. If your pacing is off, if it comes and goes, if it isn't infused with tension, then editors and readers are likely to throw your story against the nearest wall.

Your formatted outline already contains (or should contain) all of your plot sketch threads. When you completed the middle section of your story evolution worksheet in chapter four, you should have inserted all your threads.

Now that you've completed your formatted outline, you can tag (identify) each plot thread, then trace (follow) it from start to finish to make sure it's solid. In order for each thread to be strong within the written book, it must be strong in the outline. Evaluating the strength of your plot threads now can save you many rewrites in the future.

## Tagging and Tracing Your Story Goal

As you know, your story goal is your main plot thread, the one that starts in the beginning of the book and continues until the very end, involving all characters and subplot threads. You identified your own story goal when you completed the plot sketch worksheet, you clarified your story goal when you completed the story evolution worksheet, and you gave the goal context when you incorporated all your plot threads into a formatted outline. Using information from these documents to tag and trace your story goal is simple.

Start by reviewing your story goal. Then read through your scene capsules, identifying elements that further the story goal. Tag each of these elements by marking it [Story Goal]. Let's walk through an example together.

In this case, we'll return to the plot sketch we completed of Alice Sebold's *The Lovely Bones* on pages 35–36 of chapter two. The story goal, or theme in this case, is listed as: "After fourteen-year-old Susie is murdered by a neighbor, she watches from her heaven as her family, friends, and murderer live out their lives. She watches with envy and sadness as she's unable to return to them and live out her own life." Now, let's project what the first few capsules in the author's formatted outline might have looked like. For the sake of example, I've simplified the capsules so that each one represents an entire chapter, rather than a single scene within one chapter. I've also gone ahead and marked the elements in the capsules that further the story goal.

## FORMATTED OUTLINE CAPSULES
### TITLE: *THE LOVELY BONES*

| | |
|---|---|
| **Day:** | ? |
| **Chapter and Scene:** | chapter 1 |
| **POV Character:** | Susie Salmon |
| **Additional Characters:** | Mr. George Harvey (her murderer) |
| **Location:** | "the hole" where she's murdered, and her heaven |
| **Approximate Time:** | midday |
| **Facts Necessary:** | Susie was murdered on December 6, 1973 on her way home from school. |
| **Notes:** | |
| **Questions:** | |
| **Draft of Scene:** | Susie is murdered by a neighbor, someone her father had called "a character," when she's fourteen years old. |
| | Her life after death in her heaven. |

*[page break for new capsule]*

| | |
|---|---|
| **Day:** | ? |
| **Chapter and Scene:** | chapter 2 |
| **POV Character:** | Susie |
| **Additional Characters:** | those in her memories; Holly, Susie's roommate; Franny, Susie's intake counselor; Susie's father and mother; Officer Len Fenerman (on the phone); Ray Singh, the boy who had a crush on Susie |
| **Location:** | Susie's heaven, her family's home, etc. |
| **Approximate Time:** | ? |
| **Facts Necessary:** | |
| **Notes:** | |
| **Questions:** | |
| **Draft of Scene:** | Susie's memories of what she imagined high school would be like, and her dreams. **[Story Goal]** |

On her third day in heaven, Susie meets Holly, who's also been there three days. Franny comes on the fifth day. Susie's heaven grows with roads leading out, and she begins to hope that she can change the lives of those she left behind.

One of Susie's body parts is found **[Story Goal]**; her parents begin to accept—though they refuse to believe—the horrible truth that she may be dead. Her sister is told, and her sister must face the possibility of Susie's death.

The love letter put into Susie's notebook by Ray is discovered where it was carried away from the site of her murder by animals. **[Story Goal]**

Evidence continues to mount as to the certainty of Susie being dead, and Susie watches the reactions from heaven. **[Story Goal]**

*[page break for new capsule]*

| | |
|---|---|
| **Day:** | ? |
| **Chapter and Scene:** | chapter 3 |
| **POV Character:** | Susie |
| **Additional Characters:** | Ruth Connors and Ruth's mother; Susie's friends Clarissa and Brian |
| **Location:** | Susie's heaven, on the earth, Ruth's house and Susie's school |
| **Approximate Time:** | ? |
| **Facts Necessary:** | |
| **Notes:** | |
| **Questions:** | |
| **Draft of Scene:** | Susie touches Ruth—"my soul shrieked out of Earth. I could not help but graze her." Ruth believes she saw a ghost, and becomes obsessed with Susie. |
| | Susie's memories of her mother, and the one time Susie saw her as someone mysterious and unknown—not mother and wife, homemaker, gardener, or sunny neighbor. Susie's father feels her presence. |

Notice the story goal doesn't truly reveal itself until chapter two. The first chapter is generally dedicated to introducing the characters and setting the stage for the rest of the book. This is typical of most novels. It's possible to add even more story goal tags to this example, but some elements are so closely messed with subplots, that the subplot threads would need to be identified as well. In order to eliminate confusion, then, I limited the tags to ones that focus exclusively on the story goal. We'll discuss tagging subplots shortly.

When you're working on your book, remember to judge each plot thread both individually and within the context of the entire story. When does a certain thread need to be introduced? When is the best time to bring it up again? How often does it need to be touched on in order to maintain tension and reader interest?

Balancing plot threads is tricky, but it's extremely important to the development and success of any story. As you trace your story goal throughout your formatted outline, ask yourself these questions: Does my story goal develop correctly? Is the pacing steady, or does it lag? Is there any point where the conflict fizzles, or just stops altogether? Are there any rough transitions? Is the path constant, or are there holes in the course of its development? Is the development of the thread logical?

Remember that none of your plot threads should be considered minor, because all threads should work in harmony. But the plot elements *will* have varying degrees of importance. For instance, in my paranormal romance *Sweet Dreams*, one of the most essential plot threads is the telepathy between the hero and heroine. Nearly everything else in the book (from the romance thread to the story goal) hinges on this telepathy. The hero's headaches, stemming from the demon who haunts him, are also important because this plot thread helps to develop other aspects of the plot and the romance. Bottom line, though, I wouldn't consider his headaches a major plot thread. Is the headache plot thread any less important to the balance of the story than the telepathy plot thread? No. They work together.

There will be times when some of your story threads will merge, and you'll have difficulty deciding which thread is which as you tag. This is a good sign—it means that you've successfully interwoven your threads into the fabric of your story. A tangential or disjointed thread has no place in your story. You want your threads to mesh together. If you can't decide how to tag a certain thread, then use multiple tags, applying as many as necessary. Tagging and tracing is for your own use; don't make the process hard for yourself.

## Tagging and Tracing Subplot Threads

Subplot threads can be traced in much the same way as the story goal. Let's take a look at another example of this process, this time from Louis L'Amour's Western classic *The Ferguson Rifle*. We start with a list of the subplot threads that would have been completed in the preliminary outline stage.

WORKSHEET 4

PARTIAL PLOT SKETCH
TITLE: *THE FERGUSON RIFLE*

**Subplot Threads:**
1. Travel to the West is dangerous—Indians can be friendly or unfriendly. By nature, Ronan is a cautious man. While there's talk of wrongs done to the red man, Ronan is more concerned with his own scalp.
2. Captain Luis Fernandez and his Indian allies are after Ronan and his company because Fernandez doesn't realize that the Louisiana Territory has been sold to the United States by Emperor Napoleon.
3. Ronan wonders if the fire that killed his wife and son was an accident, or deliberate.
4. A dead man is found on the trail with some buttons and a map in his pockets. Treasure is rumored to be hidden all over in Western America. This man was shot because of treasure.
5. Lucinda Falvery is being hunted by the five men who killed her father, the man found on the trail. The five men are looking for the treasure on the map, and they killed Lucinda's father for it before she escaped with the boy.
6. Ripley Van Runkle, dweller in the caves, has spent ten years searching for the treasure.
7. The indication of love developing between Ronan and Lucinda.

Now, let's tag these subplot threads within the structure of a formatted outline.

FORMATTED OUTLINE CAPSULE
(WITH TAGGED SUBPLOT THREADS)
TITLE: *THE FERGUSON RIFLE*

| | |
|---|---|
| **Day:** | ? |
| **Chapter and Scene:** | chapter 9 |
| **POV Character:** | Ronan Chantry |
| **Additional Characters:** | 5 men, Lucinda Falvey, Jorge Ulibarri, 7 Indians |
| **Location:** | the West |
| **Approximate Time:** | afternoon |
| **Facts Necessary:** | |
| **Notes:** | |
| **Questions:** | |
| **Draft of Scene:** | Ronan has left the company he's traveling with to seek out the woman and boy **[SUBPLOT 5]** who were with the man who was killed. **[SUBPLOT 4]** Ronan has been searching for clues to their location for most of the day when he comes upon five men who demand to know what he's doing out there. **[SUBPLOT 5]** After telling them to mind their own business, Ronan continues his search, knowing these are the men who killed the man on the trail. **[SUBPLOTS 4 AND 5]** Ronan finds the woman and boy. **[SUBPLOT 5]** Saying his friends are further along the trail, they hurry to catch up while putting distance between them and the five men who are obviously searching for the woman and boy. **[SUBPLOT 5]** Indians are suddenly on the trail before them. **[SUBPLOT 1]** |

Ideally, if we tagged and traced the entire book, you'd be able to pull out each individual thread and evaluate its development from start to finish. That's what you're striving to do with your own outline. However, it's interesting to note that in *The Ferguson Rifle*, two of these subplot threads were never fully resolved. Subplot threads 2 and 3 were brought up several times within the book, but neither had a satisfactory conclusion. Every book should stand on its own, even when it's part of a series or has a sequel. However, as I mentioned in chapter two, subplot threads don't necessarily have to tie up neatly the way the story goal has to. With that in mind, any unresolved subplot threads can easily be addressed in a sequel.

As we also discussed in chapter two, the prominence of the romance thread varies depending on the story. In a romance novel, of course, the romance thread is as dominant as the story goal. In other genres, it's a short-term subplot thread. In *The Lovely Bones*, one romance thread (the romance between Susie and Ray Singh) begins in chapter two. This is an important thread, but it's not a dominant aspect of the overall story: We labeled it as subplot 4 on our sample plot sketch. It's important to note that this particular thread isn't mentioned again until chapter six, which includes a memory of Susie's first kiss with Ray the day she died. The relationship between Susie and Ray is bittersweet and sad, and adds intrigue to the story each time Ray is mentioned. This thread is interspersed throughout the book very carefully until the culmination of the relationship near the end of the book.

## Tagging and Tracing Tension

You can trace tension in your book just as you can trace plot threads. Tension is essential in any genre, in every single book. A quality story demands it. Your readers will demand it, too, otherwise there's no reason for them to continue turning the pages. Tension can come from many different areas, such as description, dialogue, introspection, and conflict. You can use pacing, foreshadowing, and backstory to create tension.

Remember, tension and conflict go hand-in-hand. Wherever you have conflict, you need to have tension. Because you have tagged and traced your plot threads throughout your story, you know exactly where you need to have tension. In a romance novel, where a romance plot thread is a necessity, there must be romantic or sexual tension infusing each interaction between your hero and heroine.

Look at the tagged examples throughout this chapter. Following each plot thread, you can imagine exactly where the tension needs to be. Each thread has conflict, and conflict must be infused with tension. But don't worry if you can't *feel* the tension while you review the outline. Just because the outline isn't nail-bitingly tense doesn't mean that your book won't be chock-full of suspense. In the outline, it's enough just to give yourself directions for adding tension. These directions don't have to be eloquent. You can simply *remind* yourself to include tension in the appropriate scenes in your outline, as in this example based on Marilyn Tracy's romantic suspense novel *A Warrior's Vow*.

FORMATTED OUTLINE CAPSULES
(WITH TAGGED AND TRACED TENSION)
TITLE: *A WARRIOR'S VOW*

|  |  |
|---|---|
| **Day:** | ? |
| **Chapter and Scene:** | chapter 5, scene 1 |
| **POV Character:** | Leeza Nelson |
| **Additional Characters:** | the Apache tracker James Daggert, who's helping Leeza look for a boy (Enrique) who ran away from the orphanage ranch Leeza's helping to manage |

| | |
|---|---|
| **Location:** | New Mexico |
| **Approximate Time:** | night |
| **Facts Necessary:** | |
| **Notes:** | |
| **Questions:** | |
| **Draft of Scene:** | Enrique's glove is found, indicating that Leeza and Daggert are not far behind him. **{PLOT TENSION}** Knowing the boy's horse will force him to stop for the night, Leeza and Daggert also stop and make camp. Daggert has abrasions on his wrist from the horses, and Leeza puts cream on them. **{ROMANTIC/SEXUAL TENSION}** |

Daggert tells Leeza his son was a couple years younger than Enrique when he disappeared. James found his son too late to save him from a serial killer. Daggert admits that when he takes any tracking job now, he's always searching for the man who killed his son and so many others. **{PLOT TENSION}**

Leeza wants to reach out to Daggert both emotionally and physically. They kiss. **{ROMANTIC/SEXUAL TENSION}**

A lost coyote pup howls, and they separate for the night, though when she puts her hand in his, his fingers tighten. **{ROMANTIC/SEXUAL TENSION}**

*[page break for new capsule]*

| | |
|---|---|
| **Day:** | same day |
| **Chapter and Scene:** | chapter 5, scene 2 |
| **POV Character:** | the serial killer |
| **Additional Characters:** | |
| **Location:** | between Daggert and Leeza's camp and Enrique's |
| **Approximate Time:** | later that night |
| **Facts Necessary:** | |
| **Notes:** | |
| **Questions:** | |
| **Draft of Scene:** | The serial killer is playing with his "toys"—mementos from each of his killings. He'll teach the woman and boy (Leeza and Enrique) about boundaries first, then finish with Daggert. **{PLOT TENSION}** |

# DAY 27: ISOLATING PLOT THREADS

Once you've completely tagged and traced the plot threads and tension in your outline, try reading it through and seeing if you feel more confident in judging the strength of your outline. Does each plot thread stand on its own and follow a strong course from start to finish?

If you're still not as sure as you'd like to be, there's one more step you can take, a procedure called isolating plot threads. When you isolate a particular plot thread in your outline, you should be able to see any weakness in that thread and gauge what's needed to improve it.

Isolating threads is also an ideal way to identify and get rid of a sagging middle or weak tension. A sagging middle, in blunt terms, is a lull in the middle of your book caused by a plot thread that isn't well thought-out and doesn't unfold naturally. By isolating each plot thread, you can discover exactly where the problems are and correct them.

You'll eventually become an expert at unfolding your plot threads slowly but steadily and maximizing the potential for plot tension. What's in your outline should carry over into the actual book. So if your pacing is solid in the outline, it will be solid in your novel as well.

Begin Day 27 by saving a separate copy of your tagged and traced outline. You'll isolate your plot threads from this second document so you don't mess up your tagged outline. Then create a separate document for each thread you'll be isolating. You'll wind up with files named "Story Goal" and "Subplot 3," for example.

You can take two approaches to isolating the plot threads. If you were isolating subplot 3, you could save your entire tagged outline as a new document called "Subplot 3," then delete everything not tagged as part of subplot 3. (You would also keep text tagged as plot tension resulting from subplot 3.) Do the same thing for each thread within your plot sketch. Expect this part to be even messier than the initial tagging phase, because you're really deconstructing your outline into little bits now.

Another approach would be to open your tagged outline and go through it scene-by-scene, copying each plot thread and pasting it into its own document. This method would allow you to isolate all the plot threads at the same time.

To show you how this is done, I've isolated a single thread from Sue Monk Kidd's *The Secret Life of Bees*. By reviewing the isolated subplot thread, you should get an idea as to how this particular thread was introduced, developed, and tied up in the story. In this case, the subplot thread is: "Bees come one summer and send Lily's life spinning off into a new orbit—a quest to discover all she can about her mother, who died when Lily was four. The bees lead Lily to August Boatwright." As you read, you discover that each time the bees are mentioned, Lily is about to learn or apply something new to her life. Epigraphs at the beginning of each chapter further illuminate the connection between Lily's experiences and the life of bees. In the example on the next page, I've taken out almost everything in the book that doesn't pertain to this particular subplot thread.

## PARTIAL FORMATTED OUTLINE CAPSULE
## (WITH ISOLATED SUBPLOT THREAD
## TITLE: *THE SECRET LIFE OF BEES*

**Chapter 1, Scene 1**

The bees came the summer of 1964, the year 14-year-old Lily's life irrevocably changed. Lily believes the bees were sent to her like the angel Gabriel was sent to the Virgin Mary, and that the bees set unpredictable events in motion. **[SUBPLOT THREAD #1]** {PLOT TENSION}

**Chapter 1, Scene 2**

Lily's nanny, Rosaleen, told her that bees swarm before the death of a human. Lily suddenly finds herself in a whirlwind cloud of bees, but when she runs to get her father, T. Ray, they've disappeared. **[SUBPLOT THREAD #1]** {PLOT TENSION}

**Chapter 1, Scene 5**

Lily is catching bees in a jar to prove to T. Ray that she's not making up the bees. Rosaleen tells her not to come crying to her when she gets stung. **[SUBPLOT THREAD #1]** {PLOT TENSION} Details on Lily's relationship with Rosaleen, a black woman, in a time of great racial tension.

**Chapter 1, Scene 14**

Remember how her mother couldn't kill even a roach, Lily opens the jar to let the bees out, but they won't go, "The world had shrunk to that jar." **[SUBPLOT THREAD #1]** {PLOT TENSION}

**Chapter 2, Scene 3**

The bee jar is empty when Lily is brought home by T. Ray from jail, where Rosaleen remains after being accosted by white men and arrested on her way to register to vote. T. Ray has told Lily on the way home that her mother ran off and left her ten years ago. The day she died, she'd come back only to get her things. Lily convinces herself T. Ray lied to hurt her. She hears a voice telling her that her "jar is open." She decides to leave, first getting Rosaleen out of jail. **[SUBPLOT THREAD #1]** {PLOT TENSION}

**Chapter 5, Scene 5**

In earlier scenes, it is revealed that Lily has a honey label that was her mother's: Black Madonna Honey. When Lily and Rosaleen arrive in a new town, Lily sees a jar with the same label and is led to August Boatwright. August, maker of Black Madonna Honey, teaches Lily bee-yard etiquette, telling her "send the bees love. Every little thing wants to be loved." Lily wants to be loved by August so she can stay with her. **[SUBPLOT THREAD #1]** {PLOT TENSION}

**Chapter 8, Scene 2**

While doing bee patrol, August tells Lily the problem with people: They know what matters, yet they don't choose it. Bees have a secret life no one knows about. A queen is the mother of every bee in the hive. They depend on her to keep it going. Lily feels her motherless place inside, her overwhelming guilt for her mother's death ten years ago. **[SUBPLOT THREAD #1]** {PLOT TENSION}

**Chapter 9, Scene 1**

Lily gets stung by a bee as they water the bees. Lily realizes that once you're stung, you can't change it no matter how much you complain. You just dive back in. Her life has made her want to give up, but she continues going, nevertheless, searching for the love she needs. **[SUBPLOT THREAD #1]** {PLOT TENSION}

**Chapter 10, Scene 5**

After May Boatwright's death, they drape the hives in black cloths as a symbol to ensure that she'll live again. "When a bee flies, a soul will rise." Life gives way to death, and death gives way to life. **[SUBPLOT THREAD #1] {PLOT TENSION}**

**Chapter 10, Scene 8**

The black cloths are removed from the hives so the bees won't become disoriented and unable find their way home again. In the same way, Lily's grief must not overwhelm her so she can't live again in the real world. **[SUBPLOT THREAD #1] {PLOT TENSION}**

**Chapter 14, Scene 1**

August shows Lily a hive that's lost its queen—a death sentence for the bees, who will stop work and become demoralized without a queen. Lily must find the mother inside of herself for strength and consolation. The human purpose isn't simply to love, but to persist in love. **[SUBPLOT THREAD #1] {PLOT TENSION}**

As you can tell, this subplot thread added a lot to *The Secret Life of Bees* in terms of story and character development, transitions, and pacing. The tension each time the bees are brought up keeps getting tighter and tighter as the story progresses, until it culminates at the very end of the story in Lily finding what she most needs in order to go on.

Remove any one subplot thread completely from your formatted outline, then reread the outline. Without that thread, something is missing, isn't it? Now try putting an isolated subplot thread into a different spot within the outline. Does it fit in any other place? It might. If some portion of your thread fits in more than one area in your outline, you'll need to decide where it fits *best*. Each thread should unfold logically and steadily, while still maintaining tension within the story. If you're uncertain about a subplot, move it around until you're sure you've got it in the right place.

When you isolate a particular plot thread in your outline, you should be able to see any holes in the thread. If it's lacking motivation or tension, you should be able to determine what's missing and where you should add something pertaining to this thread. If you can't, make some educated guesses and try each one until you figure out what works best. You also might try brainstorming with a critique partner if you're really having trouble. Once you have all your threads isolated, judge them critically. Then you'll be able to see if your story structure is strong as a whole.

To reinforce the method for and importance of tagging, tracing, and isolating individual plot threads within the formatted outline, I've included additional examples of all steps in this process on my Web site (www.karenwiesner.com), including the full outline (tagged and traced) for my novel *Sweet Dreams*.

At the end of Day 27, your outline should be extremely solid. If it's not, you may need to revisit your story evolution worksheet in order to figure out where your story fizzled. Incorporate new ideas and scenes into your formatted outline, then start the deconstruction process again to make sure the threads are strong from start to finish.

It may happen—once you've completed your formatted outline, tagged, traced, and isolated of your plot threads, and revised your story evolution worksheet—you discover you don't have enough subplot threads in your book. Don't be upset! Be glad you discovered the problem *before* you committed it to three-hundred-plus manuscript pages. It's *never* too late to add another layer of texture to your story. My writing partner and I realized, after outlining one of the books in our Falcon's Bend series, that we needed more suspects. We brainstormed and sketched out the plot and characters for these additional suspects. Then, using our most current day sheet, we figured out where to drop these new angles into the story. At that point, we were easily able to incorporate everything into the outline. Adding these new subplot threads greatly enhanced the novel. An outline should be flexible—certainly flexible enough to withstand even the most complex problems.

## DAY 28: SHORING UP WEAK ELEMENTS IN YOUR FORMATTED OUTLINE

On Day 28, continue shoring up weak elements in your plot. You may want to verbally brainstorm with your editor or a trusted critique partner to help evaluate the strength of your outline.

Tagging, tracing, and isolating plot threads are huge jobs. The good news is that you won't have to do this for every book. With experience, you'll be able to complete these steps in your head. The more times you go through it, the better you get. You'll eventually come to a point when you instinctively *know* whether your outline is strong enough.

I began tagging, tracing, and isolating my plot threads when I first started using an outline to write my books. I used this deconstruction process a few times, then realized I'd become adept enough to gauge the strength of my outline simply by running my finger down the high-concept blurb column of the day sheet. You should be able to do the same once you've used this method a few times. You'll know when you no longer need to tag and trace when you find yourself reading over your outline and feeling confident that you've got a solid, well-built story.

*Once you're sure your outline is complete and strong, go on to the next chapter to learn about revising your formatted outline.*

# CHAPTER 7

# Days 29–30:
# Revising Your Formatted Outline

Once you've incorporated everything into your formatted outline, you've evaluated the strength of the outline, and you believe it's complete, what's left to do?

From the beginning, we've considered the outline to be the first draft of your novel. When you've completed the first draft of your novel, it's time to revise! That's exactly what you'll be doing in this final stage of the 30-day method. Let's take a look at what this stage of the process entails.

**Stage 6: Outline Revision**

| Schedule | What to Complete |
|---|---|
| **Day 29** | Spend today reading over your outline and filling in any lingering holes.<br>• If there are any unanswered questions on your interview question list, interview the expert you've chosen; incorporate the answers you receive into the interview question list for future reference; and then drop the facts directly into your formatted outline wherever you might need them.<br>• If there are any questions remaining in your outline, research, or brainstorm to find the answers.<br>• One last time in your mind, tag, trace, and isolate your story threads, making sure they're all strong enough.<br>• Revise any remaining weak elements.<br>If you have an editor, agent, or critique partner you trust, brainstorm with that person on areas you feel are still weak. |

| Schedule | What to Complete |
|---|---|
| Day 30 | On this final day of the outlining process, spend time re-evaluating your outline.<br>• Do I have enough conflict to sustain the length and complexity of the book?<br>• Are my characters properly developed? Do they grow consistently throughout the book<br>• Is the pacing correct?<br>• Does the middle sag anywhere?<br>• Does the story unfold naturally with consistency and tension?<br>• Are my characters likable, with strong goals and sufficient motivation? |

Total: 2 days to a revised outline

## DAY 29: FILLING IN THE FINAL HOLES

In the revision stage of completing your outline, you'll be performing a multitude of tasks. You may find yourself dragging from all the effort you've put into your outline so far, but the good news is that you're almost done. Keep going!

As you work, be sure that you keep your outline current by recording corrections, revising chapter and scene numbers, and printing out clean copies of your work. Also remember to write the computer file name of each document on the first page of the hard copy so that you don't lose track of where things are. Stay organized by continuing to put project documents (including the outline, research, etc.) into your project folder.

### Incorporating Last-Minute Research

Today's agenda should keep you busy. If, on Day 25, you discovered you still needed some answers to the questions on your interview questions worksheet (Worksheet 8 in Appendix C), then you probably have an appointment with your chosen expert coming up. To prepare yourself for the appointment, review the interview question list. If you've already answered some of the questions on this list through other research, delete those from the document. Then figure out where each piece of the new information you plan to get will go in your outline. Since your outline is almost final, you will be able to figure out where this information is needed and include accurate chapter, scene, and/or page numbers directly on the interview question list. Print the revised list and put it in a folder with a pad of paper and a pencil for notes, a personal recorder with extra batteries and cassettes, and your business card or contact information to give to the person you're interviewing.

Once the interview is complete, transcribe your notes directly into your interview questions list, then print a hard copy for future reference (you'll probably need this information while you're working on editor revisions, and you may need it again for another book). Put the hard copy in the story project folder. Then incorporate the information directly into your formatted outline wherever you may need it as you work.

Let's look at an example of how interview questions and answers are used within the formatted outline. On pages 44–45 of chapter three, we looked a list of questions I came up with for an interview with a patrol sergeant for *Tears on Stone*. Here's the list again, only this time the answers have been incorporated.

## INTERVIEW QUESTIONS AND ANSWERS
## TITLE: *TEARS ON STONE*

**QUESTION 1:** How do you run a sketch that your sketch artist has done of a suspect and find a match? Do you put it in the computer with a scanner and run it through some kind of program set up for this purpose? Does a regular PD have the kind of equipment necessary to match up the sketch or do they send out for it? Do they send or fax it to DCI? If they know exactly where to look for the match, how long would it take to get the match? How long would it take if you had no idea? Who does the match? The officer looking for the information? The investigator? Patrol officer? Dispatch? What if it's a case where the suspect isn't from the area, you know who the person is, and you actually know where they're from, but you have to prove it?

**Chapter(s)/page(s) where answer is needed:** chapter 55, page 127 and chapter 56, page 130 of the outline

**Facts or information I may need during the interview:** The suspect isn't from the area, but the detectives know where she hails from.

**Answer:** We would fax it. With today's equipment, we would fax the best picture we can possibly get of this person, and we would say, "Could you help us positively identify this person?" If they couldn't do it, I would put their name with it. Problem with it is, when I feed you too much information, then you're kind of snowballing this thing for lack of a better term. I'm not going to tell you who this person is. I'm going to ask you first. Because once you start saying, "This is John Doe, this is Jane Doe and this is their brother Darrell. . . ." Now you've invited it and you don't want to do that.

Now let's look at how this information translates into a formatted outline.

FORMATTED OUTLINE CAPSULE
(WITH INTERVIEW QUESTIONS AND ANSWERS)
TITLE: *TEARS ON STONE*

| | |
|---:|---|
| **Day:** | ? |
| **Chapter and Scene:** | 55 |
| **POV Character:** | Danny |
| **Additional Characters:** | Pete, Amber, Pam, suspect |
| **Location:** | town hall and police station |
| **Facts Necessary:** | |
| **Notes:** | Sketches of a suspect are faxed to the department where it's believed the perpetrator hails from; the officer faxing this would ask if the person can be identified before offering a name; *see interview with Patrol Sergeant, question 1.* |
| **Questions:** | |
| **Draft of Scene:** | When Billie, a newcomer to Falcon's Bend, comes to the Society of Survivors meeting, Amber talks to her, finds her extremely reticent. She asks Billie (who's lied about her name) where she's from; when the woman claims she's from out of town, just passing through and heard about the meeting, Amber is instantly alerted. It's while Amber ducks out excitedly and calls Danny that she loses track of Billie and the assault on Pam happens. Amber is very hard on herself about this. She hangs up, and, a little while later, she calls Danny back. Pam has been attacked. |

Pam's assault: The meeting is over, everyone has left City Hall. Pam walks to her office three blocks away. Someone comes up in back of her (with a knife, stabs her). That person is gone when Amber shows up and finds Pam, who is alive but unconscious. There's a lot of blood, and Pam's purse contents are strewn on the sidewalk, making it look like a robbery.

Pete and Danny try to find out who the woman Amber describes is—no one recognizes her in town or outside when they ask around with her description and the false name she gave Amber.

Amber describes this woman to Danny is great detail. Danny sketches Billie, then they run the picture through the computer. When that doesn't work, going on a hunch, they fax the sketch to the Springvale Police Department, seeking confirmation of the identity of the woman without telling them who they suspect she is. Their suspicions hit pay dirt.

Once all your interview answers are incorporated, take a fresh look at your revised outline and see if any additional questions remain. Remember that your formatted outline capsule has a section for scene questions. Questions in this area should be highlighted to alert you to any holes in the outline. If you've highlighted the questions and crossed them off when they were answered throughout your outlining process, you should know in a glance what still needs to be done. Perform any research, interviews, or brainstorming necessary to fill in those holes.

## Starting the Revision Process

On Day 29, you'll also begin revising your outline. Now is *not* the time for editing and polishing. Editing and polishing are minor tasks (not in importance but in amount of work)—clean-up jobs that can include any of the following:

- rearranging sentences or scenes
- tightening sentences and individual words (such as changing passive voice to active, dull words to lively, or cleaning up repetitiveness)
- adding details or minor research
- adding a necessary scene or deleting an extraneous one
- any minor correction

You never want to start the editing and polishing process until you're sure you're done revising. Think of it this way: If you were building a house, you wouldn't start painting before all the walls were up, and you wouldn't lay carpet before the plumbing and wiring were done. Paint and carpeting are the polish of a completed room; they're the final steps to dressing it up. Writers need to concentrate on finishing a full draft of the book before endeavoring to do any editing or polishing.

## Revising the Outline Instead of the Manuscript

By creating a formatted outline, you've made the revision process much easier for yourself. You can revise the outline as much as you need to in order to fine-tune your story, and you've virtually eliminated the need to fully revise the manuscript itself later.

Sound impossible? Unrealistic? Are you wondering if it even makes sense to revise the outline instead of the manuscript?

Think of it this way: Each page of a typed manuscript has around 250 words. Therefore, a 50,000-word book will run approximately 200 pages; a 100,000-word manuscript averages around 400 pages. Your outline, on the other hand, will generally contain 1 or 2 pages per scene in an outline—1 page of the outline will equal about a 1,000 words (or more) in the book. (These are general figures.)

If you estimate that your manuscript will be about 200 pages long (approximately 50,000 words) and you end up with 50 scenes in your outline, you'll have a 50- to 75-page outline.

If you estimate your manuscript will be about 400 pages long (approximately 100,000 words) and you end up with 80 scenes in your outline, you'll have an 80- to 100-page outline.

Using these figures, we can conclude that your outline will generally be about a quarter of the size of the completed manuscript. Revising 50 to 100 pages will certainly be much easier than revising 200 to 400 pages! It just plain makes more sense to revise the outline instead of the manuscript.

On top of that, revising a completed manuscript is a horror. Any writer can attest to that, especially when he first realizes the magnitude of work that revising a draft requires. If you haven't been working with an outline, everything that happens from one scene to another affects everything else in the book. If you change something in chapter twenty-one, it may affect something—or *everything*—back in the earlier chapters. What you change in chapter eleven to match the thing you changed in chapter twenty-one can affect chapter twenty-nine. Before you know it, you're better off tossing the whole thing and starting from scratch.

If you're an unpublished author, it's going to take you a long time to finish a single manuscript working this way. Imagine if you're a *published* author, though. You've got editors waiting for you, fans to please, money to make. You can't afford to work this unproductively on any project.

Let's say you realize your timeline is off. It makes more sense now for the robbery to take place fifteen years ago instead of ten. You can use the Find/Replace function in most word-processing programs to look for "10 years" or "ten years" and replace the phrase with "15 years" or "fifteen years." (I don't recommend using the Replace All function, since you might replace your scene numbers in the process, but the Replace All function *would* work well if you're replacing one name with another, one town with another, etc.)

How about if you've reached chapter fifteen in your outline and realize there's a whole plot thread you need to explore? Think of how easy it is to drop this thread into your outline simply by using your table of contents and/or day sheet. It's never this simple in a completed manuscript.

At the end of Day 29, you might want to mentally tag, trace, and isolate your plot threads again to make sure they're strong enough. Or get together to brainstorm with an editor, agent, or critique partner about any areas you feel may still be weak.

## DAY 30: PUTTING IT ON A SHELF

The big day has arrived! The final day in your 30-day schedule is here. As I often find on this last day, there's really not much to do outside of minor editing and polishing. You may be sick to death of the outline at this point, but force yourself to go over it scene by scene one last time, asking yourself the following questions:

- Do I have enough conflict to sustain the length and complexity of the book?
- Are my characters properly developed? Do they grow consistently throughout the book?
- Is the pacing correct?
- Does the middle sag anywhere?
- Does the story unfold naturally with consistency and tension?
- Are my characters likable, with strong goals and sufficient motivation?

If your answer is no to any of these questions, you know what to do. Go back to your story evolution worksheet or deconstruct the threads to make sure each one is solid.

Once you're sure your outline is as solid as it's going to get, make any final corrections. Now is the best time to put in the actual chapter numbers, since they're unlikely to change at this stage. Make sure your table of contents also reflects any changes. Then print out a clean and fully updated copy of your formatted outline. Write the file name of the computer document on the top of the first page of the hard copy so you know exactly where to find everything when you come back to it.

Put everything necessary for this project—including the outline, all the hard copies of your research, the preliminary outline, the disk copies, etc.—into your project folder. For as long as you possibly can, put this book on a shelf and forget it.

Allowing your outlines to sit for a couple of weeks—or even months—before beginning to put everything into manuscript format is absolutely essential. The next time you pick up your formatted outline, you're going to need a fresh perspective—you'll be reviewing the outline again to be sure it is as solid as you believed it was when you finished it. The only way you'll be able to get a fresh perspective is to put your outline on a shelf, out of sight and out of mind.

Get to work on something else so you won't think about this project. When you do return to the project, plan on spending one or two weeks just reevaluating the strength of your outline before you actually start writing the book. I truly believe that authors who don't use outlines and who don't let those outlines sit for several weeks or months before revisiting them will find it hard to consistently write quality books.

---

*Your outline is completed, and you're ready for some major, well-deserved R&R to help the soil in your brain become fertile again (and to get some research done on future projects, if you can). In the next chapter, you'll learn the best to way to outline a project that's already midway through development. If you don't have any old drafts sitting around, skip ahead to chapter nine and learn how to get the most mileage out of your completed outline.*

# Creating an Outline for a Project Already in Development or Re-Outlining a Stalled Project

In this chapter, we'll be discussing the process of outlining a book for which you've already completed one or more drafts. If you're outlining a book that only has a few chapters written, you should still be able to use the outlining process that starts in chapter two. If you've already written quite a few chapters or the whole book, use the outlining process described in this chapter.

We'll also look at how to revise a manuscript draft for which you did write an outline, and how to re-outline a project that just isn't working.

## CREATING AN OUTLINE FOR A PROJECT ALREADY IN DEVELOPMENT

If you've already completed some (or all) of a manuscript draft for your project, you've probably made significant progress in developing your characters and mapping out your plot. If you're reading this chapter, however, it's a fair guess that something in the book isn't working, and you may or may not know what that something is. The instructions in this chapter will help you outline your draft so you can pinpoint problems and weaknesses and take steps to eliminate them.

Creating an outline for a book that you've already begun to write is slightly different from the process of creating an outline for a brand new idea. You'll take the steps in a different order, and the complexity of the steps will vary. The biggest difference between using the 30-day method to develop a brand new book idea and using it to outline a manuscript already in development is the time it takes. Though we're using a 30-day schedule, many of the steps in this process likely will be unnecessary for you. Skip around at your own discretion. Because of this, you probably won't need anywhere near thirty days to complete your outline.

As you work through this chapter, I'll be referring back to instruction in previous chapters. This chapter is intended to enhance, not replace, what you'll learn in chapters two through seven; the process of creating an outline for new books and those in development is ultimately very similar.

The schedule we'll be using for outlining a book already in development is as follows.

**Outlining a Book Already in Development**

| Schedule | What to Complete |
|----------|------------------|
| Days 1–3 | Evaluate the Previous Draft |
| Days 4–10 | Re-Outline |
| Days 11–12 | Miscellaneous and Closing Scene Notes |
| Days 13–14 | Character Sketches |
| Days 15–16 | Setting Sketches |
| Days 17–20 | Plot Sketch and Story Evolution Worksheet |
| Days 21–22 | Research |
| Days 23–24 | Outline Aid Worksheets |
| Day 25 | Day Sheet and Table of Contents |
| Days 26–27 | Evaluate the Formatted Outline |
| Days 28–29 | Revision |
| Day 30 | Finishing Touches |

Total: 30 days to a complete, strong, usable outline

This might look like a lot, but creating a masterpiece *does* require a great deal of work. Keep in mind that if you reach a step in the process that you don't feel you need to perform, skip it and move on to the next one. For instance, if you feel your character development is solid, there's no need to create character sketches on Days 13 and 14. Move along to the next step.

As you work through each stage, remember to consult the glossary in Appendix A if you need help with any of the terms. You may also find the step-by-step calendars in Appendix B to be useful during this process. Finally, remember to update your outline and print out a clean copy at the end of each step.

## Days 1–3: Evaluate the Previous Draft

With your story already in some form of development, you can pretty easily go over it and decide what works and what doesn't. In this situation, you'll start your outline by going through the most recent draft scene-by-scene, keeping the scenes that work and discarding the ones that don't. You'll then transform your scenes into an outline. Once you have an outline in place, you can brainstorm until you come up with stronger elements to replace the weak ones you've discarded.

I had written several full drafts of my novel *Reluctant Hearts*. The story had been with me for well over a decade, and I'd never had the time to rewrite it. I simply couldn't put it off any longer because it wouldn't leave me alone. I had about a hundred pages of notes on how to rewrite this book, with additional notes on new scenes written in longhand. I decided to sit down and outline my draft, incorporating my notes as I went. I spent almost the entire first day of the outlining process typing in my longhand notes. Although it made the process a little more difficult, I tried to type the notes in chronological order—this book was literally already mapped out from start to end in my head. I finished getting everything into the outline format that afternoon, then printed out what I'd accomplished.

I found that the outline was only a step or two from completion. Almost immediately after I had the printout in my hands, the areas that needed work revealed themselves to me. The process of typing my notes planted the story firmly in my mind and made critiquing it much easier, which is why I advised in chapter one that you write all your brainstorming notes out longhand instead of typing them as they came to you. Very late that night I went over my notes—tweaking, putting in scene breaks, and adding scenes where I needed them. The next day, I was able to put chapter numbers in place and divide the story into five parts. I also updated the computer files to reflect all I'd done the night before so I could reprint the pages and see what still needed to be done. For the rest of the week, I fleshed out scenes in the outline and did my research, incorporating what I learned into the outline the following weekend. At the end of that week, with the formatted outline of the book complete, I was ready and raring to begin writing a new draft.

I'd like to suggest a systematic, hands-on method for getting your current draft into outline form: You'll need scissors, a stapler full of staples, paper clips, and a pen. First, begin dividing the book into scenes. If you have more than one scene in a chapter, cut the pages between scenes and staple the scenes together. If the page doesn't have a page number after you cut it, write the original page number at the top of the cut page and insert an A or a B after the number so you'll know where the fragment came from. Next, paperclip the scenes together in the order in which they occur within your story and place them on a "save" pile.

Keep going until you've separated each scene. Spend the rest of Days 1–3 reading each of these scenes and making notes (either directly on the pages or in a notebook) about whether the scene is strong enough or needs work. Specify exactly what kind of work the scene might need.

If the scene doesn't seem to belong at all, write yourself a note about it (including the chapter and scene numbers), then put in into a "discard" pile, away from the scenes you'll be keeping. Don't throw anything away. You may be able to use something later.

If you feel a scene is in the wrong place, make a note about where you think it might work best. For now, put the scene into the save pile in its original position in your draft. When you finish going over the draft, try rearranging the scenes in your save pile in the order you think they need to be outlined.

As you're working on breaking down and rearranging your old scenes, make sure you're brainstorming about new scenes as well. Jot down notes about where you think any potential new scenes would fit best in the story.

At the end of Day 3, you should be ready to piece the outline together.

## Days 4–10: Re-Outline

At the start of Day 4, count up the number of scenes in your save pile. Now divide this number by the seven days in which you have to re-outline. For example, if you have seventy scenes, plan to re-outline ten scenes every day for the next seven days.

You'll be using the formatted outline capsule worksheet (Worksheet 16 in Appendix C) to incorporate these scenes into the proper outline structure. Before we continue, please flip back to pages 76–78 in chapter five. There you'll find a detailed breakdown of the capsule headings and information on how to use the worksheet to create your formatted outline document.

Once you understand how to use the scene capsules, begin incorporating the details of each scene into individual capsules (one capsule per scene), and make notes to document changes from the previous draft. Using my novel *Sweet Dreams* as an example, let's see how a scene in a draft translates into a scene capsule.

WORKSHEET 16

### FORMATTED OUTLINE CAPSULE
### (WITH REVISION NOTES)
### TITLE: *SWEET DREAMS*

**Day:** winter, around Christmas

**Chapter and Scene:** prologue

**POV Character:** villain; *change to Maddie*

**Additional Characters:** guards, cashier at drive-thru restaurant; *change to villain*

**Location:** armored van (from Wausau, WI to Milwaukee, WI); *change to Maddie's apartment, her bedroom*

**Approximate Time:** very early morning

**Facts Necessary:** *New: The villain is being transferred (from prison to prison) in an armored van from Wausau, WI to Milwaukee, WI.*

**Notes:**

**Questions:**

**Draft of Scene:** Villain is being transferred (from prison to prison) in an armored van from Wausau, WI to Milwaukee, WI. Male guards, all are heavily armed. He's thinking about Cass's daughter Maddie, wants to finish what he started last year. Cass ruined it, blocked his energy, doesn't know how he did it, but this time he won't. They drive through for breakfast (in Plover, WI); he sees the female clerk, he smiles at her.

*[Note for revision: To increase tension and make sure the book starts with high action, put this scene in Maddie's POV instead of the villain's. He's coming for her, and he warns her of this through their telepathic connection.]*

Go as far as you can putting scenes into the formatted outline document during these seven days. Work following the chronology of the story. If you're not sure about a scene—about what should come after it or about what should go into it—insert a blank capsule at this point, put in a page break, and just keeping going. You can always fill it in later.

At this stage, don't take the time to put in chapter numbers. Chapters will change often as you outline. For now, it's best just to divide your book into scenes (scene 1, scene 2, scene 3, etc.). Once the outline is revised and complete, and, therefore, it isn't likely to change much, you can add specific chapter numbers.

Also, remember to start each new scene capsule on its own page. Regardless of how much (or how little) information is in each capsule, put a page break after each one. If you're working with pen and paper, start each new scene capsule on a fresh sheet of paper and leave yourself room to expand.

At the end of Day 10, your outline should be shaping up very nicely. Once you've completed it, take a look at the outline from top to bottom. You're likely to see a lot of holes, but you'll also see a solid progression.

As we discussed earlier, each scene you write must advance the story. Every scene should add to the one before and progress the plot. Your formatted outline acts as a road map: You can see the path you must take, and you can place your scenes accordingly. It's much easier to pace your novel when it's in outline form than it would be if you just started writing the story. With an outline sketching out each scene in detail, you can tell at a glance whether each scene pushes the plot to a tight conclusion. Any scene that doesn't can be eliminated before the actual writing of the book begins.

With your formatted outline together, you now should have a good idea where the story needs work. If you can, work on filling in holes and shoring up the weak areas of the outline for the rest of Day 10.

Once you've gone as far as you can, put page numbers into the formatted outline document and print it. You can make handwritten notes on this hard copy as you work on your outline, but type in these notes and reprint the document at the end of each day.

You've done a tremendous amount of work during these last seven days, but if your mind is anything like mine, you won't be able to stop yourself from brainstorming on the book. If that happens to you, that magical element of writing is working! If it doesn't, no worries. Let yourself relax. You've still got a lot of work ahead of you.

## Days 11–12: Miscellaneous and Closing Scene Notes

On Day 11, you'll begin incorporating your miscellaneous scene and closing scene notes, along with any additional ideas you've accumulated, directly into the formatted outline. If your story has been brewing a long time since your last draft, you may have quite a few new ideas. You can read more about the preliminary outline, miscellaneous scene notes, and closing scene notes in chapter two.

## Days 13–14: Character Sketches

If, during the last twelve days, you've come to the conclusion that the problems in your story lie with your character development, be sure to complete thorough character sketches on Days 13 and 14 using Worksheet 1 in Appendix C. All the information you need for developing character sketches can be found in chapter two, pages 16–21. Once your character sketches are complete, incorporate the details into your outline. Remember to place the information wherever you might need it, even if this means recording the same information in several places. (If you're curious about why this is so important, see page 87 in chapter five.)

## Days 15–16: Setting Sketches

If you've decided your setting development is weak, be sure do thorough setting sketches (Worksheets 2A and 2B in Appendix C) on Days 15 and 16. All the information you need for completing setting sketches is in chapter two.

Once your setting sketches are complete, incorporate the details anywhere you might need them in the outline.

## Days 17–20: Plot Sketch and Story Evolution Worksheets

If you feel your plot development is weak, complete a plot sketch using Worksheet 4 in Appendix C. The plot sketch highlights the major conflicts and issues to resolve in your book. All the information you need about plot sketches is in chapter two.

The story evolution worksheet (Worksheet 5 in Appendix C) will help you plan, in great detail, how to unfurl your plot logically from start to finish. It will also assist you in monitoring character development. Keep your plot sketch in mind as you fill out the story evolution worksheet. By the time you complete it, your plot threads should be firmly enmeshed with the story evolution elements.

Once the plot sketch and story evolution worksheets are completed, incorporate the results into your outline.

## Days 21–22: Research

If you feel you need to do additional research for the book, now is the time to do it. You'll find helpful information on the research process in chapter three. If you don't feel you need any more research time, skip this step.

Once your research is complete, incorporate the information wherever it may be necessary in the outline, or include instructions on where to find the information in the notes section of your capsule.

## Days 23–24: Outline Aid Worksheets

If you find them helpful, fill out any of the outline aid worksheets (Worksheets 9–14 in Appendix C) discussed in detail in chapter three. If you don't feel you need them, don't bother with them.

Once the worksheets are completed, incorporate the information wherever it may be necessary in the outline.

## Day 25: Day Sheet and Table of Contents

On Day 25, fill out a day sheet (Worksheet 17 in Appendix C). Then, from the day sheet, create a table of contents for your outline. Instructions and guidelines for creating a day sheet and table of contents can be found in chapter five.

## Days 26–27: Evaluate the Formatted Outline

During the next two days, you'll be evaluating the strength of your outline. All the information and instruction you need for this process is included in chapter six.

## Days 28–29: Revision

For the next two days, you'll be revising the outline. Refer to chapter seven for instruction in this process.

## Day 30: Finishing Touches

Once you feel you've gone as far as you can, finalize this version of your outline and put it aside for a few weeks to gain some professional distance. If at any point you feel that something still isn't right with the book, read the sections of chapter five that talk about overcoming roadblocks (pages 95–96) on the way to a completed outline, and outlining and writing in tandem (see pages 96–97). You might also want to thoroughly review other chapters in this book, especially chapter four, which details story evolution.

## REVISING AN OUTLINED NOVEL WITHOUT STARTING FROM SCRATCH

Let's suppose that you've created a solid formatted outline, and you've written a manuscript draft based on that outline. What happens if you then realize that you have weak plot threads? Good news! You don't have to start revising the book from scratch. At least, not if you have a strong formatted outline to fall back on.

You can fix any lingering problems by using the day sheet (Worksheet 17 in Appendix C) you created after you finished your formatted outline. Please note that this method of problem solving is ideal for those times when you know—*really* know—what needs fixing in your manuscript. If you don't know what the problem is, read the novel again and make detailed notes of where things are off. If you still can't figure it out, skip to the next section in this chapter on re-outlining.

If you know where you went wrong in your manuscript, start the revision process by double-checking that your day sheet is up-to-date and matches the sequence of your book scene for scene. You may need to read (or skim) your book from start to finish to make sure the day sheet is current.

Once you're sure that your day sheet is correct, you can begin to convert it into a supplemental outline worksheet (Worksheet 18 in Appendix C). With a supplemental outline worksheet, you can isolate the exact plot threads that need to be revised or expanded.

Once you're sure your day sheet is accurate, go through it once more. Make notes on changes you think will strengthen your book. Such changes could include the following:

- rearranging scenes or chapters
- adding or deleting scenes or chapters
- changing POV
- adding or deleting characters
- adding or deleting plot threads

Once you've finished your day sheet notes, begin filling out the supplemental outline worksheet. Fill this worksheet out scene-by-scene, just as you would the day sheet. However, don't bother to fill out details for scenes that remain unchanged. Your goal at this point is not to create a new day sheet, but to list the changes you need to make to your manuscript.

If you need to reorder chapters or scenes, record them in the new order on the supplemental outline worksheet. (It's a good idea to note both the new and old chapter or scene numbers.) If you delete a scene, record it with a note that it has been deleted. If you plan to change the POV or details for a scene, note these changes in the POV Changes and Scene Detail Changes columns. Use the last column to keep track of miscellaneous notes and the effects your changes will have on other sections of the book. For instance, in *Degrees of Separation*, my writing partner and I decided to change the adoption case representative in the prologue from a woman to a man. This made a change in chapter fifty-seven, in which the case representative is interviewed about his role in the pertinent adoption. Naturally, a man's reactions are slightly different than a woman's, so we had to make notes in the comments column about those changes we needed to make.

If the changes you need to make are very minor, you can go straight to your manuscript from here. However, you may wish to return to your formatted outline, revise or create new scene capsules, and create a new day sheet to reflect the changes recorded in the supplemental outline worksheet. If the changes were particularly heavy, or if you're just not sure you succeeded in solving the problems with your manuscript, you may also choose to repeat the outline evaluation process of tagging, tracing, and isolating your plot threads.

Let's take a look at a completed supplemental outline worksheet using my novel *Degrees of Separation* as an example. When you read over the example, notice how much information comes directly from a standard day sheet.

SUPPLEMENTAL OUTLINE WORKSHEET
TITLE: *DEGREES OF SEPARATION*

| Chapter and Scene | POV Changes | Scene Detail Changes | What to Fix/ Additional Comments |
| --- | --- | --- | --- |
| prologue | Jeremy (*new*), adoption case representative | Jeremy is married, has many children (adopted and biological), and his wife is always commenting on how sensitive he is. He thinks children are a blessing, he loves them all to bits and can't imagine life without them. | Change adoption case representative to a man. Having it from a male POV will bring out stronger fear and reactions, too.<br><br>Everything else in this scene is fine. |

| Chapter and Scene | POV Changes | Scene Detail Changes | What to Fix/ Additional Comments |
|---|---|---|---|
| chapter 1 (new chapter addition) | Terry | She's walking home, feeling a little better, wondering if she did the right thing by giving in to Blaine about running away with Don. Maybe decides she's going to run away with Don after all. Plans to tell him tonight. And then someone comes up in back of her, strangles her. . . . The girl who's so close to having her dreams come true loses it all. | Chapter addition to give reader information they can't otherwise get without giving too much away |
| chapter 2 (this chapter used to be chapter one) | | | Add a note about Ben's irresistible charm with women.

Everything else in this scene is fine. |
| chapter 3 (this chapter used to be chapter two) | | | This scene is fine as is. |
| chapter 4 (this chapter used to be chapter three) | | | This scene is fine as is. |
| chapter 5 (this chapter used to be chapter four) | | End this scene when Blaine steps out of his office. | Everything else in this scene is fine as is. |

| Chapter and Scene | POV Changes | Scene Detail Changes | What to Fix/ Additional Comments |
|---|---|---|---|
| chapter 6 (new chapter addition) | Blaine | Blaine hears that the music has stopped, and this adds to his foul mood. Earlier today, this afternoon, he confronted Terry about the plans Crystal let leak that Terry and Don had of running off together. He's still ticked off about this, even though he changed Terry's mind. He thinks he nipped that potential problem in the bud. He walks out of his office and sees the cops and he's *really* ticked off now. He thinks he doesn't need this, but knows he can't show it; can't give anything away. | We find out in the new chapter one that Terry had decided to run off with Don anyway, even after Blaine's little talk to persuade her otherwise.

Blaine's obvious need to have everyone under his control makes him a suspect right from the beginning. |
| chapter 7 (not exactly new since it used to be part of chapter five) | | | Continue in Ezra's POV again with the last part of what used to be chapter five.

Everything else is as it was. |

# RE-OUTLINING AFTER AT LEAST ONE OUTLINE AND MANUSCRIPT DRAFT

There are situations in which spot fixes would require more work than re-outlining the book. This is especially true if you aren't sure what's working in your book and what isn't.

The first step in re-outlining is to make a list of all the problems you think the book has (or might have). Put your notes in the project folder, then put the manuscript on the shelf for as long as you possibly can. Take whatever steps are necessary to refresh your creativity (see the brainstorming techniques in chapter one), and allow your creative coffeepot to start brewing on the back burner as you do other things. Purge story ideas whenever you feel the need. During this break, keep thinking about the project and take notes as new possibilities come to you.

After you've gained some perspective on the work, take out the manuscript, your project folder, and any notes you made. At this point, your book qualifies as a project already in development. It's time to go back to the beginning of this chapter and follow the outlining instructions that begin on page 122.

Re-outlining and writing another full manuscript draft might sound like an immense amount of work, but in actuality you've already done most of the work. All your character and setting sketches are done (though you may need to shore them up as we've discussed), and you'll be able to use much of your previous outline and probably even many of the actual scenes you've already written. You're much better off than if you were rewriting a full manuscript that had never been outlined. If you are re-outlining because an editor requested a major revision from you, you'll now have a new outline she can read and approve; and you'll avoid having this editor send you another major revision letter—or a rejection.

Chances are, the process of outlining, writing the first draft, re-outlining and rewriting the book probably takes less time than trying to complete a solid, perfect final draft without the benefit of an outline.

Don't be discouraged if your own interest in the project periodically wanes. Simply set the book aside for a solid interval following each step in the re-outlining process. If you're on a deadline, setting aside the book might be difficult. Try to set up your schedule so you have plenty of time before the book is due.

*Once you have a full, solid outline based on previous drafts of the book, you're ready to go on to the next chapter and learn how to get the most from your formatted outline.*

# CHAPTER 9

# Getting the Most From Your Formatted Outline

Completing a full outline is one of the most exciting parts of being a writer. It's hard to describe the happiness I feel once I print and flip through my formatted outline.

As you become more familiar with the 30-day method, your speed will increase, and you'll need less time to complete each step. After repeated use of this outlining method, I've found that my mystery partner and I rarely require more than two or three weeks to research and outline a 100,000-word novel. When I'm working solo, I can complete a full outline for a mainstream romance novel of any size in a week or less. Each book in my rather complicated solo series of action adventure novels tends to take about a month, including research—possibly more when the plot is extremely complicated and major research is required. In general, the more complicated the plot, the longer it'll take you to complete the outline, but length shouldn't affect the timeframe. Because the outline is your first draft of the book, it may (and should!) take you longer to write than the first full draft of the book.

In this chapter, we're going to talk about the benefits of completing a full outline before writing the book and how to use the formatted outline to write your book.

## A SNAPSHOT OF YOUR NOVEL

The combined six stages of the 30-day method have illustrated how a complete formatted outline acts as a snapshot of your novel. It contains everything your novel will contain, only on a much smaller scale. It will be much easier to work out all the kinks in the outline than it would be in a full draft of the manuscript.

After reading your completed outline, you should feel as if you've read the entire book. While reading the outline, you should be able to see how effectively the threads mesh, how dependent they are on one another, and how they create the net that entangles the reader in the story. The book should feel complete, solid, exciting, and wholly satisfying. The characters, as well as the readers, should be so involved they simply can't afford to walk away until everything is resolved satisfactorily. A first draft outline is equivalent to the first draft of a manuscript because it reads with all the completeness and excitement of a finished novel.

You should also feel that you desperately want to write the book because it's close to completion now—the hard parts are done. When you finish the first draft of your manuscript, it should be as satisfying as a *final* draft that needs only minor editing and polishing to make it publishable.

An outline may be the bare bones of the story, but it's so complete that it qualifies as the first draft of the novel. That makes the work of actually writing the novel almost a simple process. All the hardest work—creating a strong internal structure with deep and complex plot and characters—is over.

In the five years that I've been using the outlining method described in this book, I have been steadily selling books to publishers. In all but one case, my first manuscript drafts have been the *final* drafts. At the time of this writing, I've sold all but two of the books for which I've used the method—and both of those books are currently sitting on an editor's desk. So far, all the revisions my editors have asked for have been extremely minor—basic, commonsense suggestions to refine word usage and smooth out the flow of sentences.

Using your outline as you write the full manuscript draft of your book should be so easy, you might even feel a little guilty about it. Most writers have come to believe that a solid draft of a novel can be achieved only through blood, sweat, and tears. While the 30-day method of constructing a formatted outline is designed to avoid bloodshed, you probably *have* experienced the sweat and tears—you just got all of that out of the way during the outlining process. Even if you found your first use of the outline method difficult, I encourage you to keep using it on all of your projects. I promise you that it will get easier each time.

## USING YOUR OUTLINE TO WRITE THE BOOK

Now that your formatted outline is complete, it's time to put it to use and get to work on your first manuscript draft. You probably have a million questions right now. For example, is it a bad thing if your book doesn't seem to follow your outline exactly? What, if anything, should you do if this happens? What if another story starts bugging you while you're working on this one? What if you discover you've forgotten to add something to your outline, or if you come up with a new plot thread during the writing of the book and you want to add it to the outline? What if you start to experience the symptoms of writer's block in the middle of a project? Can you revise the book while you're writing it? When should the editing and polishing take place? What do you do when you finish writing the book?

### Tweaking Your Outline as You Write

After you've allowed your outline to sit on the shelf for a while, take it down and make sure it's still solid. The truth is, most writers get so sick of a book during the process of outlining and writing that they have a hard time viewing it with impartiality. They may simply want to get away from it, so they tell themselves the book is solid enough. Sufficient shelf-time will restore your patience and interest and give you a more objective point of view. Though your outline will probably be very strong at this point, you may need to do a little layering—which involves strengthening an existing plot line by deepening characters, adding new subplot threads, or further enhancing description, dialogue, introspection, action, and tension in the story—to enhance your complexity before you begin the actual writing. Give yourself a week or two for this necessary step. You might want to use the deconstruction process in chapter six to help you reevaluate the strength of your outline afterwards.

Once you begin the writing, it's important to continue brainstorming. End each of your writing sessions by going over the next scene in your outline. You want each scene firmly in your mind before you begin writing it so you can be brainstorming in the background while you do other things. You want to keep it going around and around in your head until you're ready and raring to start writing the next day. Feel free to jot down notes at any time as the next scene is fleshed out in your mind, especially if ideas come to you in great detail.

Reviewing upcoming scenes also allows you to think about how those scenes fit into what you've just written. If your book doesn't always seem to follow your outline, yet the writing seems good to you—better perhaps than what your outline included—go with it. As you write, you'll be creating a living, breathing entity that will continue to grow on its own, in ways your outline may not account for. That's part of the magical writing element. Just make sure you adjust your full outline and/or manuscript to take new angles into account.

Even if your first manuscript draft seems to be following your outline closely, periodically go over the outline to see if your plot or characters are growing in ways that might effect scenes you haven't written yet. Read over your notes, get a good feel for what you want to do, and then make the necessary modifications. It's perfectly fine—ideal even—to write notes directly on your printed outline as you work on your novel. In fact, I'd wonder what catastrophe happened if my outline was clean when I finished writing a book!

## Purging

If a new story idea starts to bug you while you're writing, you may need to stop and take down notes about it as the ideas come to you. In fact, don't be afraid to take a day off from your current work in progress (WIP) to exorcise this new idea and send it back to your creative coffeepot. You won't be starting a new outline here—simply making notes on a future one. You need to encourage these ideas to come to you in order to keep your livelihood going strong indefinitely. Once you've purged, get back to your WIP immediately and concentrate on it. Be disciplined! If you need to refresh yourself on the purging process, flip back to chapter one.

## Final Editing Sheets

While you're writing the book, start a final editing worksheet (Worksheet 19 in Appendix C), which you'll eventually use for your final edit of the book. Use this worksheet to note anything that needs to be added, deleted, or revised in the story when you're done. You don't want to break up the flow as you write, so if you realize you forgot to add something to the outline or need to incorporate a new idea, take down a note now and correct the problem after you're done writing the first draft. Include chapter, scene, and page numbers whenever possible so you'll be able to make the corrections easily.

Take a look at the final editing worksheet I used for my novel *Waiting for an Eclipse.*

FINAL EDITING WORKSHEET
TITLE: *WAITING FOR AN ECLIPSE*

1. Establish Tommy's sense of humor more; give Steve's three kids more defined characters and voices.

2. Research the type of cat Trina is; explain why she's named Trina? (Katrina from *The Legend of Sleepy Hollow*)

3. Make Kristina wear and have more purple things.

4. Need more descriptions of:

   Kristina's apartment

   Kristina's office

   Steve's house

5. Make Steve call/talk to his sister more often (some descriptions of her personality sprinkled into these conversations); possible areas to add this to:

   chapter 3, scene 2

   chapter 6, scene 1

   chapter 9, scene 3

   chapter 10, scene 2

   chapter 14, scene 1

6. Incorporate Kristina's mother's Parkinson's Disease more; mention that she has breakfast with her mother every Friday morning at the house.

7. What kind of perfume does Kristina wear? (page 170)

8. Be more specific about the kind of drug Jessie took. (page 197)

9. What kind of teenage girl board game did Kristina and Val play? (page 234)

10. Specific skiing resorts near San Bernardino (pages 274 and 277); a restaurant in San Bernardino (page 275)

11. Last name of Steve's lawyer (page 191); very brief description of him (page 208)

12. Translate what Paul says into Spanish. (pages 275, 276)

Most of these things were minor, since I'd done almost all of my research before I outlined the book. Major changes may need to be incorporated immediately if they affect multiple parts of your book.

While writing the first draft of *Degrees of Separation*, my coauthor and I decided to give a certain suspect a handkerchief. Of course, said handkerchief would come up later in the book. Though pretty minor, the addition was essential and needed to be incorporated in several places throughout the book. I wrote some notes about it on our final editing worksheet so we wouldn't forget to incorporate the handkerchief when we were finished writing the book. I also made notes to correct all the chapters this change would affect (by reviewing our day sheet, we got a good idea where to incorporate the thread throughout the outline). I also did a bit of handkerchief research during times I wasn't writing the book, and I attached these notes to the final editing worksheet. When the book was completed and we were ready for the final edit, incorporating this thread seamlessly into the novel was simple.

Put your final editing worksheet in the folder with your outline and the rest of your reference sheets, so you have easy access to it.

## Avoiding Writer's Block

Writer's block is the inability to write. It can occur while you're in the beginning, middle, or end stages of a project. *Why* can't you write? In many cases, it's because you haven't gained full control over your muse, your creative energy. There is a way you can combat writer's block. The little-known cure: Write only what you planned to write on any given day—no more than that. This ensures you will have enough time between writing sessions to brainstorm on the next day's scene or scenes.

Does this cure sound too simple? Does it seem like too pat a solution to a widespread malady that plagues a huge chunk of the writing population? Think about it this way: Brainstorming shouldn't stop simply because you've completed an outline. It's a necessary part of every single aspect of a novel. If you write only what you *plan* to write in any given day, you give yourself sufficient time to brainstorm between sessions. The next time you sit down to work you'll have figured out how to lay out the next scene in the book and will begin writing immediately. If you're working from an outline, you'll know *exactly* what will happen in every scene, and you'll have no excuse for not brainstorming or for going blank when you sit down to write.

To avoid writer's block, write the scene you planned to write that day, then spend the rest of the day figuring out in your mind how your next scene will start, develop, and conclude. (Write details for any scenes in your outline; just don't write the actual scenes.) Work out dialogue, description, action, whatever. By all means, write all the notes you can about the upcoming scenes—just don't start writing those scenes until the scheduled time. Practicing self-discipline in this way will help you avoid writer's block, especially at that most crucial stage when you're in the middle of writing a book.

## Revising Not Allowed!

What most writers call revising is actually just editing and polishing. As we discussed earlier, editing and polishing are cleanup jobs that can include any of the following:

- rearranging sentences or scenes
- tightening sentences and individual words
- adding details or minor research
- adding a necessary scene or deleting an extraneous one
- any minor correction

As you're writing your draft, keep in mind that revision and writing are two completely different processes that require different mind-sets. Don't try to do both at the same time. Wait until you've completed the first draft of the novel before you do *any* editing or revising.

I've seen too many writers fall into the trap of starting their daily writing sessions by reading over and reworking what they wrote the day before. While it may go against everything you've learned, try *not* to go over your previous day's work. I say this because many times the process of rereading and revising can discourage you from moving forward to the next scene (i.e., it keeps you focused on the previous scene rather than the next one). Each scene has its own mood, and you need to create it from scratch each time. It's harder to create a new mood when you're still in the last one. A simple need to polish words, sentences, or paragraphs can become a complete rewrite. This isn't a productive way to work when you're attempting to *finish* the first draft of the book.

If you need to refresh yourself on what happened in the previous scene, skim your *outline* instead. Or try reading over a scene on the same day you write it and do some polishing then instead. However, the most efficient way to work is by saving all the revising and editing until the novel is complete. Don't shoot yourself in the foot.

Another unfortunate side effect of reading over your story while you're still writing it is that you don't get the necessary distance from it. If you can stop yourself from going over yesterday's material before you start writing each day, you'll enter the editing and polishing phase with fresh, objective eyes once the book is finished. It'll be as if the book has been on the shelf for a few months (or as long as it takes you to complete a draft), and you can now see the story as it really is.

When you come back to your finished novel to start the revision process, you'll rediscover your own book and you may find yourself impressed by what you've accomplished. Give yourself the time and objectivity to do that.

## Editing and Polishing: Absolutely the *Final* Step

If your formatted outline is solid, editing and polishing should be almost as simple as reading through the manuscript, making minor adjustments, and performing the tasks noted on your final editing worksheet. All books experience healthy growth through the process of writing the first full draft, so you'll probably need to do some tweaking, polishing of sentences and structure, and layering of details that create richly textured characters and plots.

The first few books you complete using the 30-day method may require more extensive editing and polishing than described above. However, the more you use the method, the less editing and polishing you'll need to do.

Ideally, wait to start the final editing and polishing process until a week or more after you've finished your final revisions. If you've set up your yearly schedule right (see chapter ten), you might even be able to set the book aside for a couple months before doing this step. I finished writing the first draft of my novel *First Love* quite literally the weekend before I was supposed to start working on an update to an annual writers reference. Since I had no time to do a final edit and polish on *First Love*, I set it aside for the three months it took to complete the nonfiction project. When I picked up the novel again, it was as if I was reading someone else's work, and I was pleasantly surprised by what I'd accomplished. The editing and polishing also seemed easier because I could see the story much more objectively than I could have if I hadn't waited.

Watching the skeleton of your outline become a walking, talking, breathing, *living* story is one of the most exhilarating experiences of being a writer. To help take you through the process of writing an outline and then completing the first full draft of your novel, I've included many goodies on my Web site for you. Be sure to visit.

## Getting Critical Reads

You've completed your novel, and you've done the revision, final editing, and polishing. Now you feel you've got a novel beyond compare. What do you do at this point? This is the time to let a small part of the world see what you've done.

Writers have a huge handicap. They can never read their books with the fresh, distanced, unbiased view that another reader has. It's time to turn your beloved opus over to a trusted spouse, critique partner, friend, or agent for a critical read.

It's a crucial time. Stephen King nailed it on the head in *On Writing* when he said, "The truth is that most writers *are* needy. Especially between the first draft and the second, when the study door swings open and the light of the world shines in."

The opinion of others is very important. You're not ready to send that book out to a publisher until you've had enough reader reactions to judge the strength of your work.

## Putting It Back on the Shelf

If you can possibly allow for more shelf-time for the final draft, do it. A couple of weeks or months will increase your ability to view the book with fresh eyes. Remember, this is your last chance to catch flaws before the book goes out to the important people who can publish it.

You might be wondering how many times you can set your book aside before it goes to an editor. I've suggested you set it aside for a few months after the outline is complete, before you begin writing the book. I've suggested you set it aside after the first draft is done, before you begin editing and polishing—and now, again, after the critical reads and before you send it off to a publisher. Like a good wine or cheese, the more shelf-time you give each book, the better it'll be.

In chapter ten, I'm going to give you specifics on how to allow all this shelf-time in your schedule without losing *any* momentum in your career. It's not only possible to be one or more books ahead of your releases (or submissions), it's the *only* way to continue your career writing several quality books a year.

---

*In the next chapter, we'll be talking about scheduling and the necessity of using goal worksheets to plot your career as a productive writer.*

# CHAPTER 10

# Outlining Your Career

If you want to be a truly productive writer, you must set goals not just for your current project, but for your career. In order to be efficient, you need a plan of action. It's never too early in your career to begin setting goals. Regardless of whether you're published, it's a good idea to plan at least a year ahead. This helps keep you forward-thinking and diligent.

If you're as yet unpublished, move on to another project after each manuscript submission. You will hone your writing with each new book you write, and one of your new projects might be your first sale. If you do sell a book, you need to have a second, "option" book waiting to show your new publisher.

Once you've sold your first book, don't sit around patting yourself on the back. Sign that contract, toast yourself with a glass of expensive champagne, and then get started on your next project immediately (if you haven't already).

By continuously moving from one project to the next, you'll develop momentum. Momentum is what keeps your career strong and moving forward. If you don't set goals and stick to them, you risk draining your momentum.

## YEARLY GOALS

One essential tool for developing and maintaining momentum in your writing career is the yearly goal sheet (Goal Sheet 1 in Appendix D). This goal sheet will help you plan the projects you'll work on during any given year. Write your yearly goals in late November or early December, so when the new year starts you know what you're going to be doing. Your yearly goals should challenge you and make you work a little harder than you think you can. And they should, above all, be flexible.

You may want your yearly goal sheet to include the dates you plan to submit a project to an agent or publisher (and to which agent or publisher). If you're already published, you can list dates you plan to submit manuscripts to the agent or editor you already have. Incorporating this project-by-project information within your yearly goal sheet helps you stay organized and on track, providing the momentum all writing careers need to sustain themselves in a tough market.

Let's take a look at the list of goals I set for myself in 1999.

## YEARLY GOALS
### 1999

✓ write *Silver Bells, Wedding Bells* novella for Mistletoe Marriages Anthology (December 1998–January 1999) (on contract, Christmas 2000 release)

✓ editor revisions for *Silver Bells, Wedding Bells*

✓ editor revisions for *Falling Star*, Book 1 of the Angelfire Trilogy (on contract, June 1999 release)

✓ editor revisions for *Flesh & Blood*, Book 2 of the Gypsy Road Series (on contract, August 1999 release)

✓ write *Fire & Ice*, Book 3 of the Gypsy Road Series (January–March) (on contract, November 1999 release)

✓ editor revisions for *Fire & Ice*

✓ sell *Electronic Publishing: The Definitive Guide* (writers reference)

✓ write *Vows & the Vagabond*, Book 4 of the Gypsy Road Series (March–June) (on contract, January 2000 release)

✓ editor revisions for *Vows & the Vagabond*

✓ write parts 2 through 4 of "Writer's Bane or Blessing" series articles for *The Write Touch* newsletter (June)

✓ prepare proposal, submit, and sell Angelfire Trilogy (Books 2 and 3) to Hard Shell Word Factory

✓ write and compile *Electronic Publishing: The Definitive Guide* (March–June) (on contract, December 1999 release)

✓ editor revisions for *Electronic Publishing: The Definitive Guide*

✓ sell *Cody Knows* (children's book)

✓ personal vacation (July)

✓ write *Sweet Dreams* (August–December)

✓ write *The Productive Writer (or How to Avoid Carpal Tunnel With All Those Revisions)* (August–December)

✓ submit *The Productive Writer* (December)

   work on *First Love* outline (Book 2, Angelfire Trilogy) (August–December)

   work on *Forever Man* outline (Book 3, Angelfire Trilogy) (August–December)

This may look like a lot, but keep in mind that:

1. The novella took less than a month to outline, write, and polish before I submitted it. (It was sold "on spec," before I even wrote a word.)

2. *Falling Star, Flesh & Blood,* and *Cody Knows* were already written in 1998 and were just awaiting editor revisions. (Editor revisions take priority for me—and should for all published authors. No matter what else I'm working on when the edits come in, I drop it and do the revisions immediately, usually completing them in a single day.)

3. The "Writer's Bane or Blessing" series articles were already written, since they'd been published previously and required very little revision.

4. I couldn't work on *The Productive Writer (or How to Avoid Carpal Tunnel With All Those Revisions)*—which was the original name for *First Draft in 30 Days*—without

working on *Sweet Dreams*, since I'd planned to use *Sweet Dreams* as the example model within *The Productive Writer*.

Therefore, I wrote five books in 1999: two romance novels, two writers reference books, and a paranormal romance. I was able to keep the momentum going in my career by completing editor revisions on books coming out that year, by working ahead of my next year's releases, and by working on new projects I planned to sell to new publishers. You'll notice by the check marks preceding entries that I accomplished everything on my goal sheet except the last two items, both of which I sold and completed in early 2000.

Whenever you write or update your annual goal sheet, try to allow for the fact that you'll be inspired by different things at different times. Allow yourself to be flexible enough to be inspired by a variety of other projects. In December 1998, when I first wrote my goal sheet for 1999, I'd included the goal to prepare a proposal for a novel called *Gilded Promises*. I later decided I was more inspired to work on either *First Love* or *Sweet Dreams*, and so I cut *Gilded Promises* from the goal sheet for the year. When you draft your goal sheet, you shouldn't feel committed to the last few items. That way you can choose the one you're most inspired to work on at the time.

Also notice that I included my vacation on my goal sheet. (I didn't end up taking more than a weekend vacation for more than two and a half years—I still cringe about how close I came to total burnout!) You need to plan your vacations as well as your active times.

You'll soon learn how to predict, down to the day, how long it will take you to complete a project. Nonetheless, there are many things that can happen to disrupt even the best laid plans. Don't forget to leave a little room for a crisis or unexpected event— an illness in the family, an exciting new sale or medium you're exploring (like a movie deal for a published novel), whatever. You can create wiggle room by adding a couple of extra projects at the end of the year that you may or may not finish, as I did in my goal sheet for 1999. Adding extra, optional projects to your goal sheet gives you room to maneuver in the direction that makes sense to you at that particular time. This flexibility also allows time to make any unplanned revisions requested by an editor, should you make a sudden sale.

You may prefer to plan your yearly goals much more loosely or even more rigorously than I do. Find what works for you. Feel free to rework your goal sheet throughout the year to take into account new projects, new sales, and new inspirations.

## MULTIYEAR GOALS

A more in-depth goal sheet may be necessary if you like to plan further ahead than one year or if you have several books scheduled for publication within the next few years. The multiyear goal sheet (Goal Sheet 2 in Appendix D) is designed to provide you with a year-by-year breakdown of your tasks and objectives so that you can allot your time intelligently.

Your multiyear goal sheet will include accurate predictions as to when you'll be working on outlines, writing books, researching upcoming projects, and allowing shelf-time for each stage of the writing process. You'll also plan time for making editor revisions of books you've sold, promoting new releases, and vacations.

Let's look at an example of a multiyear goal sheet I created for myself in early 2004.

GOAL SHEET 2

## MULTIYEAR GOALS
## 2004–2006

**January–March 2004**

Do One or More:

___ write *The Fifteenth Letter*, Book 3 of the Falcon's Bend Series, with Chris Spindler
(Quiet Storm Publishing, May 2006 release)

___ promote *Degrees of Separation*, Book 1 of the Falcon's Bend Series, with Chris Spindler
(QSP, February, May 2004 release)

**April–December 2004**

Do One or More:

___ vacation (June)

___ re-outline and/or rewrite *Mirror, Mirror*, Book 3 of the Wounded Warriors Series
(Hard Shell Word Factory, September 2004 release)

___ outline/research and/or write *Bounty on the Rebel's Heart*, Book 3 of the Incognito Series

___ editor revisions, *Tears on Stone*, Book 2 of the Falcon's Bend Series (QSP, May 2005 release)

___ editor revisions, *Mirror, Mirror*

___ promote *Mirror, Mirror*

___ begin promotional plans and revise workshops for *First Draft in 30 Days*

___ outline/research and/or write *Wayward Angels*, Book 4 of the Wounded Warriors Series
(HSWF, September 2005 release)

___ outline and write *Jewels of the Quill* anthology, Volume 1 novella

**January–December 2005**

Do One or More:

___ promotional activities for the release of *First Draft in 30 Days*

___ editor revisions, *Wayward Angels*

___ promote *Tears on Stone*

___ editor revisions, *The Fifteenth Letter*

___ editor revisions, *Wayward Angels*

___ promote *Wayward Angels*

___ outline/research and/or write *Until It's Gone*, Book 5 of the Wounded Warriors Series (HSWF, September 2006 release)

___ vacation (June)

___ outline/research and/or write *Dead Drop*, Book 4 of the Incognito Series

___ outline/research *Hard to Handle*, Book 5 of the Incognito Series

___ outline, research and/or write *Pretty Fly*, Book 4 of the Falcon's Bend Series, with Chris Spindler (QSP, May 2007 release)

___ outline and write *Jewels of the Quill* anthology, Volume 2 novella

**January–December 2006**

Do One or More:

___ promote *The Fifteenth Letter*

___ editor revisions *Pretty Fly*

___ editor revisions *Until It's Gone*

___ promote *Until It's Gone*

___ outline/research and/or write *White Rainbow*, Book 6 of the Wounded Warriors Series (HSWF, September 2007 release)

___ outline/research and/or write *Romantic Notions*, Book 5 of the Falcon's Bend Series, with Chris Spindler (QSP, May 2008 release)

___ outline/research and/or write *Hard to Handle*, Book 5 of the Incognito Series

___ outline/research *Under the Spell*, Book 6 of the Incognito Series

___ outline and write *Jewels of the Quill* anthology, Volume 3 novella

You'll notice that the beginning of this goal sheet is more specific than the end. Naturally, it's easier to calculate your schedule for the upcoming year rather than for several years down the road. At the beginning of each year (and periodically during the course of each year), take time to update your goal sheet and insert specific dates.

The multiyear goal sheet in Appendix D differs significantly from the above example because I've designed it to provide you with prompts to help you plan without missing a detail. The more familiar you become with your goal sheets, the easier it will be for you modify them to fit your specific needs.

# PROMOTIONAL GOALS

If you're a published or soon-to-be published author, a promotional goal sheet (Goal Sheet 3 in Appendix D) will help you plan for crucial promotional events, such as book signings and appearances. I use my multiyear goal sheet, as you may have noticed, to plan general periods for promotional doings and miscellaneous career activities throughout the year.

Most career authors try to do as much promotion as they can, but they may inevitably find themselves cutting back sooner or later in order to concentrate exclusively on their (financially rewarding) writing. Here's an example to get you started.

## PROMOTIONAL GOALS
## NOVEMBER 2002

| Date/Time | What | Where | Benefit | Cost |
|---|---|---|---|---|
| Nov. issue<br>Prep time: 1 hour | co-op ad with 10 other authors | *Romantic Times* magazine | review and promotion of new release | $134 (not including postage, galley, etc.) |
| Nov. 3<br>Prep time: 1 hour | complete interview | romancejunkies.com | promotion of new release | 0 |
| Nov. 5<br>Prep time: 45 min. | update my Web site for new release | eclectics.com | promotion of new release | $100 |
| Nov. 7<br>Prep time: 5 min. | query for review | Roundtablereviews.com | promotion of new release | 0 |
| Nov. 8–10<br>Prep time: 3 days (writing article and preparing for submission) | submit article | *The Writer* magazine | promotion and exposure of new release; possible payment | 0 |
| Nov. 11<br>Prep time: 2 hours | announce my contest in conjunction with my new book release | listservs, freebie sites, various Web sites | promotion and exposure of new release | 0 |
| Nov. 12<br>Prep time: 2 hours (not including travel) | book signing | Barnes & Noble | sales and exposure of new release and backlist titles | travel expenses |

| Date/Time | What | Where | Benefit | Cost |
|-----------|------|-------|---------|------|
| Nov. 21–23 Prep time: approx. 3 days | speaking at conference and participating in book signing | Writers Institute, UW Madison | promotion, sales, exposure, payment (covers lodging with small stipend) | travel expenses |
| Nov. 28 Prep time: 20 min. to prepare a introduction | live chat | Word Museum | promotion and exposure of new release | 0 |

Time spent: approximately 6 days, 6 hours and 20 minutes     Total cost: $234 + travel expenses

Your monthly promotional goal sheet will allow you to estimate the time you spend promoting and the benefits and costs associated. Of course, this helps you keep track of what you should be doing, and also lets you see if the time and money spent is justifiable.

## PROJECT GOALS

Writing and editing goal sheets can help you stay focused and see an outlined project through to completion. These goal sheets are always filled in *after* you've completed your formatted outline, and are uniquely designed to help you establish exactly how much time you need to complete the manuscript draft phase and the final editing phase. Keep in mind that your time estimates may be off the first few times you use these goal sheets, since you won't have a solid feel for how much time you'll need to write and edit. But, with practice, you'll be able to accurately gauge the average amount of time required for various writing and editing tasks. We'll go over a few tricks in the pages to come that will help you firm up your estimates.

### Writing Goals

The purpose of a writing goal sheet (Goal Sheet 4 in Appendix D) is to help you determine how much time you need to spend turning your formatted outline into a manuscript draft. To complete this goal sheet, you'll need to have a rough estimate of how much you can accomplish on a daily basis. As a general rule, writing at least one scene a day, regardless of how long or short that scene ends up, is ideal. If you're prone to writer's block, the chances of burning out or hitting a roadblock are significantly less when you're brainstorming on one scene a day instead of two or more. Furthermore, each scene must be written with its own mood and objective—it can be difficult to switch gears in the middle of your writing session when you have to move on to the next scene. If you stick to writing one scene every day, you'll rarely feel you're doing too much or too little. If your scenes are consistently too long or short, you may need to re-evaluate whether your pacing is on track, and make any necessary adjustments.

## Writing Scene by Scene vs. Page by Page

It might work best for you to write a certain number of pages a day instead of a scene or more a day. Personally, I find this method to be inefficient, though I know a lot of authors don't. If you're going strong, do you stop at 10 pages, even if you don't want to? If you're not feeling inspired at all, do you quit at 10 pages, even if you're in the middle of a scene? It would drive me crazy not to complete that scene before I quit for the day. However, if you choose to write a certain number of pages per day, your goal sheet would be based on the projected length of the book. The chart below will help you estimate the number of pages in your complete manuscript based on the number of words you're shooting for:

(estimated 250 words per page)
50,000 words = 200 pages
60,000 words = 240 pages
70,000 words = 280 pages
80,000 words = 320 pages
90,000 words = 360 pages
100,000 words = 400 pages

Therefore, if you estimate your book will be 50,000 words and you want to write 10 pages a day (not taking holidays or weekends into account), your goal sheet might look something like this:

1/2: write 10 pages
1/3: write 10 pages
1/4: write 10 pages
1/5: write 10 pages

Test yourself for a week or a couple weeks by writing however many pages you can and taking notes on what you accomplish each day. At the end of the time, figure out your average number of pages per day. Then add a page or two to your daily page goal to challenge yourself.

It might sound impossible to accurately predict how long it'll take you to complete a project, especially down to the day (assuming life doesn't throw you any radical curves). But there is a method for doing just that that anyone can use. You need to complete the following steps before you can make your prediction:

1. Develop a solid idea of how much you're able to write per working day. (This method works best if you write scene by scene rather than page by page.)
2. Determine whether you'll work weekends or holidays, and what your schedule (personal, writing, and your other job, if you have one) is like for the time period in which you'll be working on this particular book.
3. Complete a formatted outline, with scenes divided.

First, make sure you allow the outline sufficient shelf-time before you begin writing. Next, plan to give yourself at least a week or two before you start writing to go over your outline and make sure it's still solid.

Using the writing goal sheet (Goal Sheet 4 in Appendix D) and your formatted outline, make a list of the scenes within the book, putting one scene on each line. Obviously, these scenes will come from your formatted outline. You can simply make a sequential list of scenes, as shown below:

scene 1

scene 2

scene 3

Or you can specify chapter and scene number:

chapter 1, scene 1

chapter 1, scene 2

chapter 2, scene 1

chapter 2, scene 2

Figure out how many working days you'll have in a month. (I generally don't write on weekends, so for me, most months amount to approximately twenty working days.) Now, get out your calendar or planner—whatever you use to schedule your days. Any standard calendar of the upcoming months will work, but if you have events (dentist appointment or whatever) planned during the time you'll be working, you'll want to take that into account on your writing goal sheet.

Decide the date you want to begin writing and mark it down on your writing goal sheet next to the first scene. If you're writing one scene per day, you will then write the next date by the second scene, etc. Don't forget to skip weekends and holidays if you don't plan to write on those days.

8/9:    prologue

8/10:   chapter 1, scene 1

8/11:   scene 2

8/12:   chapter 2, scene 1

8/13:   scene 2

By the time you've put a date next to each scene in your book, you know exactly when you'll be done with the first draft.

It's my experience, after outlining and writing close to 50 novels, that an outline will be approximately a quarter of the size of your finished novel. There certainly can be a wide variance because every project is different and some authors write consistently short or long scenes. The list below is an estimate of how the number of scenes in an outline will translate to novel length, assuming there are roughly 250 words per page:

up to 20 scenes in an outline = a novella-length work of 7,000–15,000 words

30–40 scenes in the outline = 50,000–75,000 words

41–70 scenes in the outline = 76,000–90,000 words

71 or more scenes in the outline = 100,000+ words

Here are some examples of how I figured out my own schedule estimations:

*Vows & the Vagabond*

- 46 scenes at 20 working days per month
- 2 months, 6 days to write an 80,000 word novel, not including editing, polishing, and proposal
- budget 2½ to 3 months for project completion

*No Ordinary Love*

- 68 scenes at 20 working days per month
- 3 months, 8 days to write a 90,000 word novel, not including editing, polishing, and proposal
- budget 3½ to 4 months for project completion

*Tears on Stone*

- 74 scenes at 20 working days per month
- 3 months, 14 days to write a 110,000-word novel, not including editing, polishing, and proposal
- budget 4 months for project completion

You'll notice I budgeted some extra time at the end of the writing process for editing and polishing. We'll discuss these steps later in the chapter.

As soon as an outline is complete, you can work up a writing goal sheet, taking into account shelf-time and a week or two for outline review and revision. You can then translate the information from your writing goal sheet directly into your yearly goal sheet.

**Yearly Goals With New Writing Goal**

| WHAT I want to accomplish | WHEN I want to accomplish it |
|---|---|
| Write *Tears on Stone* | March 8–June 8 |

We talked earlier about a multiyear goal sheet. Accurately estimating the time you'll spend on various projects will be very helpful when you're filling out your yearly and multiyear goal sheets.

But remember: Being productive should not mean being rushed. If a story needs more time, give it all it needs—*as long as you continue to meet your daily goals.* If you're a beginner, you may need to be more flexible, but having personal goals can help you no matter what stage you're in. Should you find that you're daily goals make you feel rushed, take time to evaluate whether you're trying to do too much. Would one scene per day be more managable for you than two? Be more flexible with yearly goals than daily goals.

## Editing Goals

An editing goal sheet (Goal Sheet 5 in Appendix D) allows you to accurately predict how long it will take you to edit and polish your completed manuscript.

The principle here is the same as for a writing goal sheet, only this time you know, based on your completed manuscript, the exact number of pages in your novel. First, decide how long you can afford to let the book sit on the shelf after you've finished the first draft. Then decide how much time you have to perform the edits. Two weeks is the maximum amount of time it takes me to do a final edit and polish. I spend one week marking the edits on the hard copy of the book, then I take a few days to make corrections to the computer file. I spend the rest of the second week making sure the book is sufficiently ready to submit to an editor by giving the book one last proofread. When you've used this method a few times, your editing and polishing should require only a week or two as well.

Start by dividing the number of pages in your book by the number of days you've allotted yourself for editing. An editing goal sheet might look something like this one, which I created for one of my novels, *No Ordinary Love.*

## EDITING GOALS
### TITLE: *NO ORDINARY LOVE*

**Page Count of Final Manuscript:** 400

**Time Allotted for Editing:** 5 days; 80 pages per day

**Deadline for Submission:** September 1

| Date | Scene(s) or Pages to Edit |
|------|---------------------------|
| August 5 | 80 pages |
| August 6 | 80 pages |
| August 7 | 80 pages |
| August 8 | 80 pages |
| August 9 | 80 pages |

**Days for Computer Corrections:** 3 days (approximately 133 pages per day); August 10–13

**Days for the Final Polish:** 1 day; August 14

**Days for Critique From Partners:** 1–3 weeks; August 15–28

**Days for Corrections From Critique and Preparing Proposal:** 2–3 days; August 29–31

**Target Date for Sending Out:** September 1

On this example, I included a target date for submitting a query letter and synopsis of the project to agents and editors. I needed to do several things before I sent the book out: finish the editing and polishing; make corrections within the document on my computer; allow sufficient time for my critique partners to give me their gut reaction to the book; and make any corrections to the book before preparing the proposal. Because I had everything scheduled and followed the steps chronologically, I was able to meet my target submission date with time to spare, and I knew the quality of the proposal would be high, since I took the necessary time to do each step right.

## GETTING AHEAD AND STAYING THERE

Once you become a published author, the pressure is on at all times. It never lets up because you're expected to go one better every time. You'll put as much pressure on yourself as your publishers and readers do. That's why it's absolutely essential to become a productive writer as soon as you can—ideally, *before* you sell your first book. You'll be confident about what you can do, and you'll have more to offer any publisher who contracts for your books.

A good rule of thumb for unpublished writers is to stay one or two projects ahead of your *submissions.* If you're a published author, you should stay one or two projects ahead of your *releases*. Three to six months before a new year, you need to be thinking—or preferably *working*—on next years' projects.

So how exactly do you get ahead? It won't be something you can do overnight. It may take you a year or longer to get the pattern firmly established. If you want to get ahead, using completed outlines to write novels, allowing shelf-time for each step, and setting goals will lay the groundwork. The next thing you need to do is evaluate how goal-oriented you are and whether you can complete projects on time. If your answers to those evaluations are negative, take it slow. Try to sneak in one extra outline a year, then allow that outline to sit until you've got plenty of time in your regular schedule to work on the book.

If you're the type of writer who has one or more story ideas in the works and completes projects on time or well in advance, you're ready to shift your career into high gear. Figure out your schedule in advance by filling out a multiyear goal sheet. The first year of that sheet should be much more detailed than the rest. Plan to outline all the stories you want to write the next year at or before the beginning of that year, then allow those outlines to sit for several months before you begin writing one of them. Or, alternate between projects that are in different stages of development. Just keep moving forward.

It's *never* too early in your career to get ahead. Start now, and in a year or less, you'll have a disciplined, well-constructed career that stays strong indefinitely.

---

*As we've seen, there's no wrong way to write a book—but there are ineffective ways of writing.*

*Use the method contained in this book until it becomes instinctive to you, until you almost feel guilty about how easy it is for you to write a wonderful novel no one can put down.*

*Dare greatly, writer. Everything you need is within your grasp. If you're willing to take up the challenge, success is just around the corner.*

# Glossary

**action:** the advancement of plot and subplot threads from scene to scene.

**aftereffects of resolution:** an emotional reaction or an event that carries a plot or subplot thread beyond its resolution.

**alibi worksheet:** a chart of all suspects in a mystery or suspense novel and their alibis; used by the writer to keep facts straight while working.

**black moment:** the bleakest moment in the book, where the reader is lead to believe the main character's future may never be happy because the obstacles appear monumental. Both characters and reader are convinced the story goal can never be achieved. The black moment comes at the end of the middle section of the book.

**brainstorming:** creative ''brewing'' of an idea where stories come to life in spurts.

**capsule:** formatted outline capsules contain single-scene summaries. Each capsule contains the day; the chapter and scene numbers; the point-of-view character; additional characters; the location and time; any facts, notes, or questions necessary to the development of the scene; and, finally, the draft of what happens in the scene.

**character sketch:** details about a character, including physical descriptions and mannerisms, personality traits, background, internal and external conflicts, occupation and miscellaneous facts.

**closing scenes:** in the preliminary outline, closing scenes notes are ideas about your story's final scenes that you know go into the end of the book, but it's too early to determine exact placement.

**conflict:** the opposition to the happy resolution of story goal; the clash between good and evil that motivates the main characters to act.

**consistency:** the steady flow of each plot and subplot thread from the beginning of the book through the middle to the resolution.

**contrast:** a method for building action and suspense by providing baffling, opposed characteristics in characters, setting, descriptions, and dialogue.

**crime timeline:** an outline aid that provides an account of how a crime was committed, by whom, the exact time and place, and possible witnesses to the deed; used by the writer to keep facts straight during the outlining process.

**day sheet:** a reference sheet that tracks the day of each scene, the point-of-view (POV) character, and the number of POV scenes for each character. Also contains a high-concept blurb to summarize the scene; used to track the consistency of the plot. The day sheet has many other uses as well, including as the table of contents in the formatted outline and as a supplemental outline sheet when revising an outline or manuscript.

**deconstructing the outline:** tagging and tracing all plot threads within a formatted outline from beginning to end, then isolating those plot threads to ensure they develop to their full potential.

**description:** in-depth details about characters and settings that allow the reader to use the full range of his senses.

**dialogue:** words spoken (external) or thought (internal monologue) by a character.

**dialogue worksheet:** an outline aid that lists each character's way of speaking; used to keep facts straight during the outlining process.

**downtime:** a point at the end of the middle section of the book in which the main character takes release from the action to reflect on what happily-ever-after could have been. During downtime, the main character believes that the story goal is unachievable and he will seemingly give up the fight.

**draft:** either the initial full writing of a manuscript or a start-to-finish overhaul of a manuscript.

**editing:** making small changes in an outline or manuscript.

**editing goal sheet:** a goal sheet prepared after the completion of the first draft of the book that includes a schedule for editing the book.

**exorcising:** writing down stray ideas on other projects so you can focus on your current work in progress (WIP). All purged ideas go into the story project folder where they belong.

**fact sheet:** a list of important character and setting details; used to keep facts straight during the outlining process.

**final (or second) draft:** using the *First Draft in 30 Days* method, the second (or final) draft of your book will be the first actual writing of the book—the flesh on the bones of the outline. The first draft of the book is your completed *outline*.

**final editing worksheet:** a running list of changes that must be made into a draft once the draft is complete.

**"first draft" outline:** an outline so complete that it actually qualifies as the first draft of the book since it contains everything a draft would contain (the bones of the story) on a much smaller scale. The first draft outline is also referred to as a snapshot of your book.

**flashback:** a memory or description of a pivotal event that occurred previous to the current story timeline; used to build suspense, slow down the action, provide missing details, illuminate hidden motivation, or reveal an answer to a mystery.

**foreshadowing:** a method for building action and suspense by hinting at what is to come.

**formatted outline:** the final version of your outline, including your preliminary outline, research, story evolution worksheet, outline aid worksheets, and a table of contents. A formatted outline is ideally the first draft of your novel, and is written scene by scene in formatted outline capsules.

**genre:** the category or type of book (e.g., mystery, romance, fantasy).

**interview question list:** a list of questions that you need answered (either by doing book research or talking to a professional in the field) in order to complete your outline.

**introspection:** a character's observation of her own mental or emotional state, or thoughts of the situations she faces.

**isolating plot threads:** viewing tagged and traced plot and subplot threads individually, away from the rest of the outline, to ensure each one develops to its full potential.

**layering:** strengthening an existing plot line by deepening characters, adding new subplot threads, or further enhancing description, dialogue, introspection, action, and tension in the story.

**linear writing:** working chronologically and progressively from beginning to end, scene by scene.

**long-term threads or goals:** the story goal (and, in a romance novel, the romance thread). Long-term threads in your story are the goals that all your main characters are fighting for.

**miscellaneous scene notes:** ideas you have about a story that don't fit chronologically into the summary outline, or ideas that you might want to explore later but aren't sure really belong in the story.

**mood:** the feeling or atmosphere of a scene, carefully constructed through description, dialogue, introspection, and action. Mood often elevates suspense.

**motivation:** something that drives the main characters to relentlessly pursue a satisfactory, happy resolution to the story goal.

**multiyear goal sheet:** an aid for planning your writing goals several years in advance.

**nonlinear writing:** working out of order or skipping around during the process of building your story structure. The opposite of working in chronological order.

**omnipresent point-of-view (POV):** the reader is privy to all characters' viewpoints at the same time. In other words, the reader can be in any character's head at any time throughout the story.

**pacing:** the rate at which each plot and subplot thread progresses from the beginning of the book, through the middle course of the book, to its satisfactory resolution.

**plot sketch:** a document outlining the story goal and subplot threads, including tension, release, downtime, the black moment, resolution, and aftereffects of resolution.

**polishing:** once the final draft is complete and editing is done, polishing is the rearranging of sentences or scenes, tightening of words and sentences, and any minor bit of correction that finishes the book.

**preliminary outline:** the foundation of your story, including character, setting and plot sketches, a summary outline, miscellaneous scene notes and closing scene notes, research, outline aid worksheets, and a story evolution worksheet.

**project folder:** a large folder containing all the materials relevant to a specific novel or book idea.

**promotional goal sheet:** a document for the planning and scheduling of promotion goals for a given month.

**purging:** writing down stray ideas on other projects so you can focus on your current work in progress (WIP). All purged ideas go into the story project folder where they belong.

**release:** any temporary easement of either romantic/sexual tension or plot tension. Release must be immediately followed by action to build the suspense back up and keep the reader interested.

**re-outlining:** going through the outlining process after writing a full draft in order to strengthen the weak areas.

**research list:** a list of areas that need to be researched for a particular story.

**resolution:** the satisfying, logical conclusion of long-term and short-term plot threads.

**revision:** making significant changes to an outline or draft, such as adding or deleting plot threads or completely rewriting certain sections.

**romance thread:** a dominant romantic and/or sexual relationship between the main characters that is as important to the story as the story goal and functions as a long-term plot thread. A minor romance plot thread is considered a subplot thread rather than a long-term thread.

**romantic/sexual tension:** any type of suspense or exaggerated awareness that brings the romance thread to a fever pitch of anticipation.

**sagging middle:** a lull in the middle of a story caused by weak plotting or pacing.

**setting sketch:** details and descriptions of the various locations and time periods in a story.

**shelf-time:** a period of time during which you allow the story to sit on a shelf without working on it. Shelf-time gives you a fresh perspective on the material when it's time to revise.

**short-term threads or goals:** the subplot threads that make up a novel, usually translating into short-term quests toward the resolution of the story goal.

**story evolution:** the careful, systematic unfolding of plot from the beginning of a novel to the end; the basic framework of an outline.

**story goal:** the major, long-term plot thread that continues from the beginning of the book until the very end. Every subplot thread and all characters are involved in achieving the story goal.

**subplot threads:** the short-term conflicts or goals that make up a novel, usually translating into short-term quests toward the resolution of the story goal.

**summary outline:** in the preliminary outline, the summary outline is the first attempt to set down the basics of what happens in the book, starting from the beginning and moving from scene to scene chronologically.

**supplemental outline worksheet:** a document that helps to isolate plot threads so they can be fixed or layered to strengthen the story.

**suspense (or tension):** the sensation of uncertainty and anticipation in the reader.

**tagging:** identifying all the plot threads within the formatted outline.

**tension (or suspense):** the sensation of uncertainty and anticipation in the reader.

**theme:** the dominant idea driving the story; story goal and theme can be used interchangeably when it comes to outlining.

**threads:** plots and subplots.

**timelines:** documents that help keep track of the major events and character backgrounds within your story; used to keep facts straight while working.

**tracing:** following the course of plot threads from start to finish in the formatted outline.

**writing goal sheet:** a specific daily schedule of writing goals.

**yearly goal sheet:** a document for planning your writing schedule during any given year.

# 30-Day Method Schedules

## 30-DAY METHOD SCHEDULES
## FOR NEW PROJECTS

| Overview Schedule | Stage | Total Days | Tracking Your Days | Notes |
|---|---|---|---|---|
| Days 1–6 | Stage 1: Preliminary Outline | 6 | | |
| Days 7–13 | Stage 2: Research | 7 | | |
| Days 14–15 | State 3: Story Evolution | 2 | | |
| Days 16–24 | Stage 4: Formatted Outline | 9 | | |
| Days 25–28 | Stage 5: Outline Evaluation | 4 | | |
| Days 29–30 | Stage 6: Outline Revision | 2 | | |

Total: 30 days to complete

1

| Schedule | What to Complete | Notes |
|----------|------------------|-------|
| Day 1 | Character Sketches | |
| Day 2 | Setting Sketches and Research List | |
| Day 3 | Plot Sketch | |
| Days 4–5 | Summary Outline | |
| Day 6 | Miscellaneous Scene Notes and Closing Scene Notes | |

Total: 6 days to complete

STAGE 2

| Schedule | What to Complete | Notes |
|----------|------------------|-------|
| Days 7–13 | Research your book and complete any outline aid worksheets you need. | |

Total: 7 days to complete

STAGE 3:
STORY EVOLUTION

| Schedule | What to Complete | Notes |
|----------|------------------|-------|
| Days 14–15 | Fill out the Story Evolution Worksheet | |

Total: 2 days to complete

## STAGE 4:
## FORMATTED OUTLINE

| Schedule | What to Complete | Notes |
|---|---|---|
| Day 16 | Using the formatted outline capsule worksheet, incorporate your preliminary outline (including the summary outline and plot and character sketches), your miscellaneous scene notes, and your closing scene notes into a scene-by-scene formatted outline. | |
| Day 17 | Incorporate story evolution worksheet information into your formatted outline. | |
| Day 18 | Incorporate character and setting sketches throughout your formatted outline. | |
| Day 19 | Incorporate your research into your formatted outline. | |
| Days 20–23 | Brainstorm to fill out the formatted outline based on the length and complexity of the story. | |
| Day 24 | Create a day sheet and a table of contents. After revising, add chapter numbers and print out your outline. Finally, go over the hard copy, layering and strengthening the story. | |

Total: 9 days to complete

| Schedule | What to Complete | Notes |
|---|---|---|
| Days 25–26 | Tag and trace your threads. | |
| Day 27 | Isolate each plot thread. | |
| Day 28 | Revise weak elements. | |

Total: 4 days to complete

STAGE 6:
OUTLINE REVISION

| Schedule | What to Complete | Notes |
|---|---|---|
| Day 29 | Spend today reading over your outline and filling in any lingering holes.<br>• If there are any unanswered questions on your interview question list, interview the expert you've chosen; incorporate the answers you receive into the interview question list for future reference; then drop the facts directly into your formatted outline wherever you might need them.<br>• If there are any questions remaining in your outline, research or brainstorm to find the answers.<br>• One last time in your mind, tag, trace, and isolate your outline threads, making sure they're all strong enough.<br>• Revise any remaining weak elements.<br>• Add chapter numbers if you haven't done so already.<br>If you have an editor, agent, or critique partner you trust, brainstorm with that person on areas you feel are still weak. | |
| Day 30 | On this final day of the outlining process, spend time re-evaluating your outline.<br>• Do I have enough conflict to sustain the length and complexity of the book?<br>• Are my characters properly developed? Do they grow consistently throughout the book?<br>• Is the pacing correct?<br>• Does the middle sag anywhere?<br>• Does the story unfold naturally with consistency and tension?<br>• Are my characters likable, with strong goals and sufficient motivation?<br>Once you've entered in any final corrections, print out your outline and put everything into your project folder. Then, put the manuscript on the shelf for as long as possible to gain some distance from the project before continuing. | |

Total: 2 days to complete

# 30-DAY METHOD SCHEDULES
# FOR BOOKS IN DEVELOPMENT

| Schedule | Steps to Complete | Total Days | Tracking Your Days | Notes |
|---|---|---|---|---|
| Days 1–3 | Evaluate Previous Draft | 3 | | |
| Days 4–10 | Re-outline | 7 | | |
| Days 11–12 | Miscellaneous and Closing Scene Notes | 2 | | |
| Days 13–14 | Character Sketches | 2 | | |
| Days 15–16 | Setting Sketches | 2 | | |
| Days 17–20 | Plot Sketch and Story Evolution Worksheet | 4 | | |
| Days 21–22 | Research | 2 | | |
| Days 23–24 | Outline Aid Worksheets | 2 | | |
| Day 25 | Day Sheet and Table of Contents | 1 | | |
| Days 26–27 | Evaluate the Formatted Outline | 2 | | |
| Days 28–29 | Revisison | 2 | | |
| Day 30 | Finishing Touches | 1 | | |

Total: 30 days to complete

## DAYS 1–3:
## EVALUATE THE PREVIOUS DRAFT

| Schedule | What to Complete | Notes |
|----------|------------------|-------|
| Days 1–3 | Go through the most current draft of the book scene by scene to figure out all the parts that worked in the overall concept of the story. Brainstorm throughout this process to come up with stronger ideas to replace the weak. | |

Total: 3 days to complete

| Schedule | What to Complete | Notes |
|---|---|---|
| Days 4–10 | Count the number of scenes in the previous draft and divide this number by 7 days. Re-outline the resulting number of scenes per day. | |

Total: 7 days to complete

DAYS 11–12:
MISCELLANEOUS AND CLOSING SCENE NOTES

| Schedule | What to Complete | Notes |
|----------|------------------|-------|
| Days 11–12 | Incorporate any new scenes or data into the formatted outline. | |

Total: 2 days to complete

## DAYS 13–14:
## CHARACTER SKETCHES

| Schedule | What to Complete | Notes |
|----------|------------------|-------|
| Days 13–14 | Create character sketches and incorporate them into your formatted outline. | |

Total: 2 days to complete

## DAYS 15–16:
## SETTING SKETCHES

| Schedule | What to Complete | Notes |
|----------|------------------|-------|
| Days 15–16 | Create setting sketches and incorporate them into your formatted outline. | |

Total: 2 days to complete

DAYS 17–20:
PLOT SKETCH AND STORY EVOLUTION WORKSHEET

| Schedule | What to Complete | Notes |
|---|---|---|
| Days 17–20 | Create a plot sketch and then a story evolution worksheet and incorporate them into your formatted outline. | |

Total: 4 days to complete

DAYS 21–22

| Schedule | What to Complete | Notes |
|----------|------------------|-------|
| Days 21–22 | Perform research and incorporate it into your formatted outline. | |

Total: 2 days to complete

DAYS 23–24:
OUTLINE AID WORKSHEETS

| Schedule | What to Complete | Notes |
|----------|------------------|-------|
| Days 23–24 | Fill out relevant outline aid worksheets and incorporate them into your formatted outline. | |

Total: 2 days to complete

| Schedule | What to Complete | Notes |
|---|---|---|
| Day 25 | Prepare a day sheet and incorporate it into your outline as the table of contents. | |

Total: 1 day to complete

## DAYS 26–27:
## EVALUATE THE FORMATTED OUTLINE

| Schedule | What to Complete | Notes |
|----------|------------------|-------|
| Days 26–27 | Tag, trace, and then isolate your plot threads. Ask a critique partner, agent, or editor to help you evaluate the strength of your outline. | |

Total: 2 days to complete

DAYS 28–29

| Schedule | What to Complete | Notes |
|----------|------------------|-------|
| Days 28–29 | Revise your outline, asking yourself the following questions:<br>• Do I have enough conflict to sustain the length and complexity of the book?<br>• Is the pacing correct?<br>• Does the middle sag anywhere?<br>• Does the story unfold naturally with consistency and tension?<br>• Are my characters likable, with strong goals and sufficient motivation? | |

Total: 2 days to complete

DAY 30:
FINISHING TOUCHES

| Schedule | What to Complete | Notes |
|----------|------------------|-------|
| Day 30 | Make computer corrections and update or insert chapter and page numbers if you haven't already.<br> Print your outline, put everything into your project file, and put this book on the shelf as long as you possibly can. | |

Total: 1 day to complete

# 30-Day Method Worksheets

CHARACTER SKETCH
TITLE:

Character Name:

Nickname:

Birth Date/Place:

Character Role:

PHYSICAL DESCRIPTIONS

Age:

Race:

Eye Color:

Hair Color/Style:

Build (Height/Weight):

Skin Tone:

Style of Dress:

Characteristics/
Mannerisms:

PERSONALITY TRAITS:

BACKGROUND:

INTERNAL CONFLICTS:

EXTERNAL CONFLICTS:

OCCUPATION/
EDUCATION:

MISCELLANEOUS NOTES:

GENERAL SETTING SKETCH
TITLE:

**Name of Setting:**

**Characters Living in Region/Time Period:**

**Year or Time Period:**

**Season:**

**City and State:**

**Miscellaneous Notes:**

CHARACTER SETTING SKETCH
TITLE:

**CHARACTER NAME:**

**GENERAL SETTINGS FOR
THIS CHARACTER:**

**CHARACTER'S HOME
SURROUNDINGS:**

**City or Town:**

**Neighborhood:**

**Street:**

**Neighbors:**

**Home:**

**Home Interior:**

**CHARACTER'S
WORKPLACE:**

**City or Town of Business:**

**Business Name:**

**Type of Business:**

**Neighborhood:**

**Street:**

**Individual Workspace:**

**Co-workers:**

**MISCELLANEOUS NOTES:**

RESEARCH LIST
TITLE: _____

**Material to research for the book:**

1.

2.

3.

4.

5.

6.

7.

8.

9.

10.

PLOT SKETCH
TITLE:

**Story Goal:**

**Romance Thread
(Optional):**

**Subplot Threads:** 1.

2.

3.

4.

5.

6.

7.

**Additional:**

**Plot Tension:**

**Romantic/Sexual Tension:**

**Release:**

**Downtime:**

**Black Moment:**

**Resolution:**

**Aftereffects of Resolution:**

SUMMARY OUTLINE
TITLE:

**A free-form chronological summary of all introductory scenes for the book:**

## MISCELLANEOUS SCENE NOTES
TITLE:

**A free-form summary of scenes appearing in the middle portion of the book:**

CLOSING SCENE NOTES
TITLE:

**A free-form summary of scenes appearing in the closing portion of the book:**

## INTERVIEW QUESTIONS
### TITLE:

**Interviewee:**

**QUESTION 1:**

**Chapter(s)/page(s) where answer is needed:**

**Facts or information I may need during the interview:**

**Answer:**

**QUESTION 2:**

**Chapter(s)/page(s) where answer is needed:**

**Facts or information I may need during the interview:**

**Answer:**

**QUESTION 3:**

**Chapter(s)/page(s) where answer is needed:**

**Facts or information I may need during the interview:**

**Answer:**

DIALOGUE SHEET
TITLE:

**Character:**

**Dialogue specifics:**

**Other mannerisms or character tags:**

**Character:**

**Dialogue specifics:**

**Other mannerisms or character tags:**

**Character:**

**Dialogue specifics:**

**Other mannerisms or character tags:**

**Character:**

**Dialogue specifics:**

**Other mannerisms or character tags:**

**Character:**

**Dialogue specifics:**

**Other mannerisms or character tags:**

FACT SHEET
TITLE:

| Page or Chapter | Character | Location | Fact |
|---|---|---|---|
| | | | |
| | | | |
| | | | |
| | | | |
| | | | |
| | | | |
| | | | |
| | | | |

BACKGROUND TIMELINE
TITLE:

| Page or Chapter | Character | Age/Year(s) | Background Facts |
|---|---|---|---|
|  |  |  |  |
|  |  |  |  |
|  |  |  |  |
|  |  |  |  |
|  |  |  |  |
|  |  |  |  |
|  |  |  |  |
|  |  |  |  |

MISCELLANEOUS TIMELINE
TITLE:

| Page or Chapter | Character | Location | Timeline Fact |
|---|---|---|---|
| | | | |
| | | | |
| | | | |
| | | | |
| | | | |
| | | | |
| | | | |

CRIME TIMELINE
TITLE:

| Page or Chapter | Character/ Suspect | Location at the Time of the Crime | Day and Time | Specific Information |
|---|---|---|---|---|
| | | | | |
| | | | | |
| | | | | |
| | | | | |
| | | | | |
| | | | | |
| | | | | |
| | | | | |

MOTIVES AND ALIBIS
TITLE:

| Suspect | Motive | Alibi |
| --- | --- | --- |
|  |  |  |
|  |  |  |
|  |  |  |
|  |  |  |
|  |  |  |
|  |  |  |
|  |  |  |
|  |  |  |

STORY EVOLUTION
TITLE:

**PART I: THE BEGINNING**

**1. Conflict Is Introduced**

Detail the major conflict:

**2. Story Goal Is Introduced**

Detail the major story goal:

**3. Characters Are Outfitted for Their Tasks**

List and briefly describe the characters who will be involved in reaching the story goal and defeating the conflict. Detail each character's strengths and weaknesses:

1.

2.

3.

Additional:

**PART II: THE MIDDLE**

**1. Characters Design Short-Term Goals to Reach the Story Goal**

Character 1:

Briefly describe first short-term goal and how character will reach it:

Character 2 (Optional):

Briefly describe first short-term goal and how character will reach it:

Additional Characters (Optional):

Briefly describe first short-term goal and how characters will reach it:

**2. Quest to Reach the Story Goal Begins**

Briefly detail the events that take place:

**3. First Short-Term Goals Are Thwarted**

Briefly detail the events that take place:

**4. Characters React With Disappointment**

Character 1:

Briefly describe reaction:

Character 2 (Optional):

Briefly describe reaction:

Additional Characters (Optional):

Briefly describe reaction:

### 5. Stakes of the Conflict Are Raised

Detail new stakes of the conflict and how they affect all subplots:

### 6. Characters React to the Conflict

Character 1:

Briefly describe reaction to the conflict:

Character 2 (Optional):

Briefly describe reaction to the conflict:

Additional Characters (Optional):

Briefly describe reaction to the conflict:

### 7. Characters Revise Old or Design New Short-Term Goals

Character 1:

Briefly describe new short-term goal and how character will reach it:

Character 2 (Optional):

Briefly describe new short-term goal and how character will reach it:

Additional Characters (Optional):

Briefly describe new short-term goal and how characters will reach it:

### 8. Quest to Reach the Story Goal Is Continued

Briefly detail the events that take place:

### 9. Short-Term Goals Are Again Thwarted

Briefly detail the events that take place:

### 10. Characters React With Disappointment

Character 1:

Briefly describe reaction:

Character 2 (Optional):

Briefly describe reaction:

Additional Characters (Optional):

Briefly describe reaction:

### 11. Stakes of the Conflict Are Raised

Detail new stakes of the conflict and how they affect all subplots:

### 12. Characters React to the Conflict

Character 1:

Briefly describe reaction to the conflict:

Character 2 (Optional):

Briefly describe reaction to the conflict:

Additional Characters (Optional):

Briefly describe reaction to the conflict:

\* *Items 7 through 10 can repeat here. This section of the cycle can repeat several times throughout the course of your novel as your characters readjust their short-term goals in order to meet their objectives.*

### 13. Downtime Begins

Detail the events that lead to downtime:

Character 1:

Briefly describe reaction to these events:

Character 2 (Optional):

Briefly describe reaction to these events:

Additional Characters (Optional):

Briefly describe reaction to these events:

### 14. Characters Revise Old or Design New Short-Term Goals With Renewed Vigor

Character 1:

Briefly describe desperate short-term goal and how character will reach it:

Character 2 (Optional):

Briefly describe desperate short-term goal and how character will reach it:

Additional Characters (Optional):

Briefly describe desperate short-term goal and how characters will reach it:

### 15. The Quest to Reach the Story Goal Continues, But Instability Abounds

Briefly detail the events that take place:

16. **The Black Moment Begins**

Briefly detail the events that take place and how they affect all subplots:

17. **The Characters React to the Black Moment**

Character 1:

Briefly describe reaction:

Character 2 (Optional):

Briefly describe reaction:

Additional Characters (Optional):

Briefly describe reaction:

## PART III: THE END

1. **A Pivotal, Life-Changing Event Occurs**

Detail this event and how it affects all subplots:

2. **Characters Modify Short-Term Goals One Last Time**

Character 1:

Briefly describe final short-term goal and how character will reach it:

Character 2 (Optional):

Briefly describe final short-term goal and how character will reach it:

Additional Characters (Optional):

Briefly describe final short-term goal and how characters will reach it:

### 3. The Showdown Begins

Showdown details (including all main characters who are involved):

### 4. The Opposition Is Vanquished and the Conflict Ends

Details:

### 5. The Story Goal Is Achieved

Detail resolution plot and all subplots:

1.

2.

3.

Additional:

### 6. Characters React to the Resolution of the Plot and Subplots

Character 1:

Briefly describe reaction to the end of the conflict:

Character 2 (Optional):

Briefly describe reaction to the end of the conflict:

Additional Characters (Optional):

Briefly describe reactions to the end of the conflict:

**7. The *Relationship* Black Moment Is Addressed (Romance Novels Only)**

Character 1:

Briefly describe reaction:

Character 2 (Optional):

Briefly describe reaction:

**8. Characters Revise Their Life Goals**

Character 1:

Briefly describe life goal:

Character 2 (Optional):

Briefly describe life goal:

Additional Characters (Optional):

Briefly describe life goals:

**9. Possible Reemergence of the Conflict or Opposition**

FORMATTED OUTLINE CAPSULE
TITLE:

Day:

Chapter and Scene:

POV Character:

Additional Characters:

Location:

Approximate Time:

Facts Necessary:

Notes:

Questions:

Draft of Scene:

DAY SHEET
TITLE:

| Day | Chapter and Scene | POV | Total POVs for Character | High-Concept Blurb |
|-----|-------------------|-----|--------------------------|--------------------|
|     |                   |     |                          |                    |
|     |                   |     |                          |                    |
|     |                   |     |                          |                    |
|     |                   |     |                          |                    |
|     |                   |     |                          |                    |
|     |                   |     |                          |                    |
|     |                   |     |                          |                    |
|     |                   |     |                          |                    |

SUPPLEMENTAL OUTLINE
TITLE:

| Chapter and Scene | POV Change | Scene Detail Changes | What to Fix/ Additional Comments |
|---|---|---|---|
|  |  |  |  |
|  |  |  |  |
|  |  |  |  |
|  |  |  |  |
|  |  |  |  |
|  |  |  |  |
|  |  |  |  |
|  |  |  |  |

FINAL EDITING
TITLE:

**Areas that need to be added, reworked, or deleted when the first draft of the manuscript is complete:**

1.

2.

3.

4.

5.

6.

7.

8.

9.

10.

# 30-Day Method Goal Sheets

## YEARLY GOALS
YEAR:

**WHAT I want to accomplish**

**WHEN I want to accomplish it**

1.

2.

3.

4.

5.

6.

7.

8.

9.

10.

## MULTIYEAR GOALS
### YEARS:

**Year:**

**Contracted Releases:**

Publisher:

Title:

Editor Deadline:

Release Date:

Outline: from _____ to _____

Shelf-Time: from _____ to _____

Full Draft: from _____ to _____

Shelf-Time: from _____ to _____

Editor Revisions: from _____ to _____

**Uncontracted Projects:**

Title:

Genre:

Intended Completion Date:

Intended Submission Deadline:

Submit To:

Outline: from _____ to _____

Shelf-Time: from _____ to _____

Full Draft: from _____ to _____

Shelf-Time: from _____ to _____

**Uncontracted Project(s) (Optional):**

Title:

Genre:

Intended Completion Date:

Intended Submission Deadline:

Submit To:

Outline: from _____ to _____

Shelf-Time: from _____ to _____

Full Draft: from _____ to _____

Shelf-Time: from _____ to _____

## PROMOTIONAL GOALS
### MONTH OF _____, 20___

| Date/Time | What | Where | Benefit | Cost |
|-----------|------|-------|---------|------|
|           |      |       |         |      |
|           |      |       |         |      |
|           |      |       |         |      |
|           |      |       |         |      |
|           |      |       |         |      |
|           |      |       |         |      |
|           |      |       |         |      |
|           |      |       |         |      |
|           |      |       |         |      |
|           |      |       |         |      |

**Time spent** _____          **Total cost** _____

WRITING GOALS
TITLE:

| Date | | Scene(s) or Pages |
|------|---|-------------------|

1.

2.

3.

4.

5.

6.

7.

8.

9.

10

EDITING GOALS
TITLE: _____

**Page Count of Final Manuscript:**

**Time Allotted for Editing:**

Days for Computer Corrections:

Days for the Final Polish:

Days for Critique From Partners:

Days for Corrections From Critique and Preparing Proposal:

Target Date for Sending Out:

**Deadline for Submission:**

# Index